STEWART MARKER, FALL IN!

25 November 1997

Mary Jean Stewart

*To
Alan Fellows,
critic and encourager.*

STEWART MARKER, FALL IN!

MARY JEAN STEWART

M&N PUBLISHING
HUDDERSFIELD

© Copyright 1996
Mary Jean Stewart

The right of Mary Jean Stewart to be identified as the author of this work has been asserted by him in accordance with the Copyright, Designs and Patents Act 1988.

All rights reserved. No reproduction, copy or transmission of this publication may be made without written permission. No paragraph of this publication may be reproduced, copied or transmitted save with the written permission or in accordance with the provisions of the Copyright Act 1956 (as amended). Any person who does any unauthorised act in relation to this publication may be liable to criminal prosecution and civil claims for damages.

First published in 1996 by M & N Publishing Co. Ltd
3 Lion Chambers, John William Street, Huddersfield HD1 1ES

Bound and Printed in Great Britain by
Edgar Woffenden Printers, Birkby, Huddersfield

Designed by Ian Chatterton
975 Leeds Road, Deighton, Huddersfield HD2 1UP

Paperback   ISBN 1 899865 90 X

CONTENTS

	PROLOGUE	7
PART I	THE WRENS JUNE 1944–OCTOBER 1946	9
	Chapter 1	10
	Chapter 2	12
	Chapter 3	16
	Chapter 4	19
	Chapter 5	22
	Chapter 6	25
	Chapter 7	29
	Chapter 8	32
	Chapter 9	35
	Chapter 10	40
PART II	ROYAL INFIRMARY, EDINBURGH 1948–1950	43
	Chapter 1	44
	Chapter 2	47
	Chapter 3	52
	Chapter 4	53
PART III	LAGOS, NIGERIA MARCH 1955–JULY 1956	57
	Chapter 1	58
	Chapter 2	62
	Chapter 3	64
	Chapter 4	69
PART IV	LONDON, ONTARIO & NEW YORK 1957–1961	73
	Chapter 1	74
	Chapter 2	77
	Chapter 3	80
	Chapter 4	83

PART V	THE CONGO 1961–1964	*91*
	Chapter 1	*92*
	Chapter 2	*95*
	Chapter 3	*99*
	Chapter 4	*102*
	Chapter 5	*106*
	Chapter 6	*109*
	Chapter 7	*111*
	Chapter 8	*114*
	Chapter 9	*116*
	Chapter 10	*120*
	Chapter 11	*122*
	Chapter 12	*125*
PART VI	**ROME 1965**	*129*
	Chapter 1	*130*
	Chapter 2	*133*
PART VII	**TEHRAN 1967**	*135*
	Chapter 1	*136*
	Chapter 2	*139*
	Chapter 3	*143*
PART VIII	**SENEGAL 1968**	*147*
	Chapter 1	*148*
	Chapter 2	*150*
	Chapter 3	*153*

PROLOGUE

STEWART MARKER, FALL IN!

"Is this your first visit to a lunatic asylum, Miss Stirling?" asked my father, strolling round the grounds of Whittingham Hospital with the young woman to whom he'd just been introduced. 22-year-old Agnes Stirling was horrified. From a sheltered background she'd had no idea the 33-year-old son of her mother's old friend was a doctor in that sort of hospital.

A year later Roy Stewart and Agnes became engaged. Twelve months after that they were married and the following three years saw the births of Desmond, Margaret and Mary. There was a short breather before Tom completed the family in 1930.

After Desmond was born, Daddy, as we always called him, became Medical Superintendent of a London County Council mental hospital in Leavesden near Watford. He didn't put up for long with the house provided for his use: a grim little villa built in yellow brick to match the hospital, although its gothic windows were innocent of the iron bars that made the hospital resemble a prison. Intending to have a large family my father persuaded the Council to buy Coles Farm, a six-bedroomed Edwardian house one mile down the road.

When we were small the garden surrounding the house seemed vast. Immensely satisfying it was too with lawns, orchards and vegetable garden and rough places for our games of sentry and hide and seek. Down by the tennis court stood a cherry tree from whose outstretched branch hung a rope. Up and down this we climbed, pretending to be Tarzan. In the small patch of open ground next to the summer-house lay a small swimming-pool, constructed with the help of patients from the hospital.

Having once been part of a farm the property was well supplied with outhouses, one of these serving later as workshop for the Superintendent's hobby of making things, sailing boats in particular.

When we tired of our own garden we had the run of the hospital farm and grounds. In fact, with the almost daily company of William and Margaret, brother and sister from nearby Abbots Langley (until we all went to boarding school we neither had nor wanted any other friends) we enjoyed an Enid Blyton childhood, complete with obligatory pipe-smoking father smelling of tweed and a comfortably-built mother. It was from this background that I set off on my first Adventure by joining the Wrens.

Part I

THE WRENS
June 1944–October 1946

CHAPTER 1

Adjusting the angle of my knitted turban I glanced out of the third-class carriage window as the train puffed its way into Euston Station. Scrawled on a wall black with soot, the words "Second Front now" caught my eye.

Commuting between Watford Junction and Euston while undertaking a nine-month secretarial course I'd often noticed these words – "Put there by the Communists" explained one of the regulars on the train. And on the occasions when I'd turned my mind to it I'd marvelled at the courage of the Russian people enduring the bitter assaults inflicted on their nation by the German armies. Russian-made sagas depicting Leningrad's heroic citizens with their defenders clad in high-necked tunics and calf-length boots were often to be seen on our cinema screens. It was these people who were losing patience over their allies' slowness in starting up a second front that would force the Germans to turn their attention elsewhere.

On this particular morning, however, my thoughts were on the exams I was to take that day at St James's Secretarial College. Snug in the dark blue coat my mother had chosen for me at Swan & Edgar's (the red wool coat I'd coveted she'd rejected as being vulgar), I stepped off the train into a cold wind to make my way to college.

The exams in shorthand and typing went well, while the one in bookkeeping did not. The books balanced but the answers were wrong. However, having passed in the other subjects I was eligible for a job at the Foreign Office. Such an occupation would have been regarded by those in power as representing the 'work of national importance' in which everyone had to be employed upon reaching the age of 18. But that would have meant being a civil servant, conjuring up in my mind an image of lacy jumpers and baggy tweed skirts. Not for me, thank you. As soon as I was seventeen-and-a-half I'd be a Wren.

Some weeks later the second front became a reality. On the 6th June 1944 the Allies launched their invasion into Normandy. Towards the end of the same month my sister Margaret and I joined up. Round about this time a frightening new weapon made its debut from across the channel: the pilotless bomb, quickly given by the British the cosy nickname of doodlebug. The first time I heard one pass overhead, the alien sound filled me with dread, while the next time I mistook it for a small aircraft with engine trouble. Bracing myself for the crash I sent up a prayer: "Please God let the pilot escape even if he's a German."

Speeding along a few hundred feet above the ground the doodlebug produced an ugly, ragged noise until its engine cut out: then there was silence. This was the moment at which the monster had been programmed to tip up and drop to earth with its cargo of high explosive.

To a certain extent we became accustomed to the sight and sound of these evil objects overhead, but I always nursed the craven hope the thing would carry on a little further before going quiet. Shame would then follow: if it wasn't to land on me, it was going to land on someone else.

For the Stewart sisters, however, there was by then the prospect of a new adventure to concentrate on. Our choice of the Women's Royal Naval Service had been arrived at for two good reasons: one, both grandfathers had served in the Royal Navy and two, the uniform was becoming. We had written off for and received application forms; on them were listed the categories of work offered. To be part of a Wren boat's crew was the ambition of many girls but I'd put down "despatch rider" and, for second choice, "air mechanic".

When summoned for interview it was disappointing to be told the quota for despatch riders had long since been filled and to be an air mechanic you needed maths, not amongst the subjects featured on my School Certificate.

What the WRNS needed was girls to carry out confidential work at Wren establishments in Middlesex. The officer with two rings on her sleeve couldn't give any details of these 'Special Duties X' but had obviously made up her mind several of us were suitable candidates, so who were we to demur. (Margaret heard afterwards we'd been chosen partly because we'd been to boarding school "Where you damn' well do as you're told".)

Saddened by the news that we wouldn't be stationed anywhere near the sea, we were, however, intrigued to know we'd be doing something secret. In due course we were to learn to call ourselves P5 Wrens, HMS Pembroke V being the name of the shore establishment where it all started. But first of all we must spend three weeks in Scotland learning how to be Wrens.

As promised we soon received call-up papers, rail vouchers and instructions for catching the night train to Glasgow and beyond on the 28th June. Training was to be carried out at Tulliechewan Castle, or

HMS Spartiate II as it had become known for the duration of the war.

So that we had something to read, Daddy took us to Foyles second-hand bookshop where he bought a copy of "The Cloister and the Hearth" for Margaret and for me "Old St Paul's". We'd much rather have had Picture Post, Life or Lilliput to take on the journey but didn't like to ask Daddy for mere magazines.

Armed with books and suitcases we made our way to Euston. There at the dimly-lit buffet, drinking mugs of tea and eating currant buns, were other girls being seen off by their parents. We spoke to a girl with glossy, dark hair and rosy cheeks; she'd come from Swindon with her father. We took to June straight away and eventually the three of us became Best Friends.

Daddy saw us into our third-class compartment and, with touching faith in the man's ability to do anything about it in the densely-packed train, asked the guard to keep an eye on us, slipping him half a crown as he did so. Having accomplished what he could to guarantee our safe arrival at the other end, he kissed us good-bye and left to catch his own train back to Watford.

CHAPTER 2

The overnight train to Glasgow was crammed with service men and women; Margaret and I found ourselves wedged between soldiers and ATS girls in the Third Class carriage. As we travelled along one of the young women commiserated with us over the fact that Probationer Wrens had a lot of skivvying to do during their training. Although this proved to be true we were to find the experience surprisingly enjoyable.

In spite of the crush, the heat and the reek of cigarette smoke I managed to doze for most of the journey, half-waking at a blacked-out station to hear the words "This is Carlisle" echoing through the dark. A few hours later we were at Glasgow where we spilled out onto the platform and caught a local train to Balloch.

Thankful to have reached our destination and in need of breakfast, we were greeted at Balloch station by WRNS Petty Officers. They formed us into a column, three abreast. Carrying suitcases and feeling silly we walked the short distance to the camp. There we were divided into three divisions. Those of us whose surname began with an R and S or a T became members of Lynx Division. We were then taken to where we were to sleep: Nissen huts, semi-circular, corrugated-iron structures equipped with double-decker bunks for thirty or forty girls. These huts were referred to as cabins; the recreation room as the fo'c'sle and the kitchen as the galley. If there was a nautical word for anything we quickly learnt to use it.

Not yet entitled to wear the complete uniform, we were issued with dark blue, short-sleeved dresses named bluettes, black lace-up shoes, black stockings, and hats similar to those worn by matelots. (It was not done to refer to naval ratings as sailors.) For a small sum, we bought no-nonsense underwear, including 'black-outs'. These knickers were described in the clothing list as being "in directoire style, closed at the knee". Accustomed to such garments Margaret and I and others equally unsophisticated didn't mind wearing black-outs.

A perk designed to save us all at least half a crown a month was our free sanitary towels. Our benefactor, so it was said, was Lord Nuffield.

The rain being on more often than off in this part of Scotland, we were given oilskins, sou'westers and Lancashire clogs for the duration of our stay at Tulliechewan. With wooden soles and black leather uppers fastened at the side with metal clasps, the clogs were excellent for squelching through the wet from one part of the camp to another.

The ATS girl on the train had been right: several hours a day were devoted to cleaning our quarters, the least rewarding task being to scrub the bare boards of the fo'c'sle deck with cold water and no soap. Once a week it was Lynx Division's turn to get up at 5.30 and spend an hour before breakfast washing down the deck of the officers' wardroom in the Castle. For this, buckets of hot water and soap were provided. A Petty Officer showed us how to work up a thick lather before spreading it about on the boards. A brisk scrub followed and then the whole mess was mopped up with a large rag: a satisfying process .

We were given lectures on both WRNS and naval customs and hierarchy. Also explained were some facts of life. For example, contrary to the warnings of our mothers we were told it wasn't possible to catch VD through sitting on a public lavatory seat. Further advice concerned the sort of drink to ask for at parties. Knowing that many of us were probably inexperienced in these matters, First Officer recommended gin and lime for its pleasant taste. She was right. It was much more agreeable than the dry sherry we'd had at home on special occasions.

Squad drill played a major part in our training and we who'd recently left schools where team games and gym featured daily took to it with enthusiasm.

Assembling on the parade ground we'd wait in our respective divisions to be formed into squads. The Stewart sisters happened to be among the taller girls and this meant one or other of us was every now and then chosen to be marker – she, who upon hearing the Petty Officer's command, sprinted up to a spot on the asphalt there to stand to attention. Next would come the words "Dressing by the right in three ranks, Lynx Division, fall in!" The others would then run up to form three long lines, one behind the other, the marker standing at the top left-hand end. With a shuffling of feet and left arm placed on the right shoulder of the girl next to you, the three lines would straighten. On the command, we'd turn left, ready to march off three abreast.

Each time I heard the call "Stewart marker, fall in!" I'd be overcome by a feeling of quite unmerited importance.

The zeal we applied to our practices became ever more pronounced as the day of the drill competition approached. Naturally we were going to win, but Lynx Division had a problem: a 40-year-old who'd joined up to serve as a cook. As well as being to our mind extremely old, she was unable to march in step. She simply walked along in her own time. Even when placed in the middle of the squad we felt she represented a serious handicap for our division. And so determined were we to come first that we tried to think of a small accident – nothing too nasty, of course – as a result of which she'd be put out of action on the day. We couldn't think of anything. But in spite of this hopeless (and unsuspecting) non-marcher, Lynx Division won.

Up the hill from our part of the camp stood the Castle. More baronial hall than castle in the English sense, it overlooked a courtyard known to us as the Quarter Deck. White lines on the tarmac indicated the dimensions of this significant piece of ground. During one of our lectures we'd been told Royal Naval tradition demanded that people going aboard must salute the quarter deck as they clambered over the side. The custom dated back to the days when a crucifix was carried in that part of the ship.

Some days after our arrival I had occasion to go up to the Castle. As I passed the first white mark I saluted and kept my hand up until I was approaching the other mark, yards away. Many times at the cinema I'd observed how it was done: the officer in the newsreel marching in front of his men, maintaining his salute until well past the admiral or general on the receiving end.

I was about to complete my march-past when a Leading Wren came panting up behind me.

"You don't need to keep your hand up as long as that, dear. Three seconds is quite enough."

My gratitude for her explaining that this rule applied even when crossing the revered quarter deck was equalled by relief that as far as I could tell no one else had witnessed the spectacle.

The Probationer Wrens had come from all over Britain, many from schools similar to Margaret's and mine, and many from less posh ones, as they put it. Some girls became so homesick after the first few days they were allowed to return home. If they'd reached the age of 18 they'd then have to find some other sort of war work. To my surprise, having always suffered from homesickness at boarding school, I didn't miss home at all. Excitement at being part of the war effort probably helped, as did the fact that there was no lack of young men to go out with.

Several of us took the bus to Glasgow on a Saturday afternoon; a dance for service men and women was being held at Green's Playhouse. Quick-stepping round the floor to the music of Joe Loss and his orchestra, I mentioned to my partner, a Petty Officer, that my sister and I hoped to be sent overseas; anywhere, we weren't fussy.

"I hope you won't be. Wrens sent overseas get spoilt rotten."

An unfortunate consequence, but a risk I was prepared to take. By the end of this our second week we'd graduated to wearing the complete uniform of double-breasted jackets with black buttons bearing the fouled anchor emblem of the Royal Navy, straight skirts, white shirts and navy ties. The hitherto unadorned hat sported a ribbon with the initials HMS embroidered on it; the small bow at the side had been tied for each Wren by an anonymous matelot.

Of the two suits we'd been issued with, one fitted well and the other didn't. The latter, of hairier material than the former, was worn only when the tiddly suit had to go to the cleaners, tiddly being naval parlance for something attractive or neat. Particularly pleasing were our navy-blue sling handbags. I'd never possessed a new one before although I'd been proud of the dowdy but good-quality leather bag my grandmother let me have when I was training to be a secretary.

Round our waists were webbing belts with small purses attached. Inside these we kept an identity card. And to be carried at all times in the breast pocket of one's jacket was a paybook containing personal details, category of employment, grade, and name of next of kin. It was an offence to carry the thing in one's bag.

At pay parade each Wren would march up to the paymaster when her name and number were called out, stand to attention and receive the money onto the outstretched paybook. Our pay amounted to thirty shillings for two weeks, although this increased to £4 a month once the real work started.

With the three-week training accomplished, Margaret, June and I, and a group of other fully-fledged Wrens journeyed south to Eastcote in Middlesex to report to the establishment known as HMS Pembroke III.

CHAPTER 3

The Wrennery was built of prefabricated one-storey buildings joined together by corridors, the linoleum floors of which were kept to a high gloss by Wren stewards. They too suffered from disappointment at being stationed far from the sea.

"Wish we could be doing this for matelots" one young steward sighed as she pushed the polisher back and forth.

At the end of one of these corridors and guarded by military police stood the entrance to a complex of huts surrounded by high walls. This was where the mysterious activity went on. The day after our arrival at Eastcote we were taken through by a Wren Petty Officer. These huts were similar in shape to the ones in which we slept and ate, but the windows were different: small, and set close to the ceiling. No one on the outside could see what was going on inside.

Petty Officer sat us down at tables in a small lecture room. Each of us was given a document headed "Official Secrets Act". This we must sign since what we were about to be told must never be divulged. Our job was to operate code-breaking machinery.

Before a feeling of anti-climax could set in (what was new about decoding, we wondered) she described the system known as Enigma. Devised by the Germans, this method of sending and receiving secret codes was of such complexity its inventors were confident no one would ever be able to crack it. They were therefore using it constantly, oblivious of the fact that the Allies had for some time been busy intercepting and decoding the messages transmitted.

It took little imagination to appreciate the advantage to the Allies of being able to read enemy messages or the resulting disaster if through someone's careless talk the Germans discovered their system had been rumbled. Therefore, when family and friends asked us what we were doing in the Wrens we must say it was "secretarial work of a confidential nature".

(Most people accepted this explanation but Margaret and I had a brother, a pacifist, whom it was difficult to fool, since he could almost read our minds. He startled me one day when he observed,

"I believe you're decoding."

"Oh, Desmond!"

I hated seeing his hurt expression when I scoffed at the absurd idea).

Our Petty Officer went on to tell us how during the early days of the war one of the encoding machines had been stolen by Allied commandos during a raid across the Channel. The purpose of the raid was well disguised, the commandos making sure the building housing the machine was totally destroyed. They'd been ordered to make sure no clues were left that might indicate to the Germans an Enigma machine had been taken. And needless to say no enemy witnesses could be left alive to give the game away.

Frustration and anguish sometimes arose when knowledge gained through the system couldn't be used even though by acting on it Allied casualties might have been avoided. The dilemma came about when only through intercepting a coded message could we have got hold of certain information; by making use of it we'd have alerted the Germans to the fact their system had been breached. With a few adjustments they could then have made sure it was impenetrable.

The genius largely responsible for working out how the messages were fed through the encoding machines and then how to decipher them was, according to our instructor, a Polish officer. We heard nothing of the Englishman Alan Turing who decades later we discovered had had more than a little to do with it.

Impressed by all we'd been told we were then taken to a room containing oblong machines roughly the size and shape of large bookcases. A primitive sort of computer (a word unknown to us in 1944), these objects were referred to as bombes and the results they produced were checked on small machines not unlike typewriters sitting in another part of the room.

The fronts of the bombes contained three banks of three rows of coloured metal drums. The drums were open at the back to reveal hundreds of little wire brushes all leaning the same way. Each brush represented a letter of the alphabet.

Our instruction began with groups being handed wheel orders and menus. The wheel order indicated which drums – red, blue, green or yellow – were to be fixed into which bank and at what setting.

The back of the bombe housed sockets, also marked with individual letters. Into these had to be inserted long, thick leads with plugs at both ends. Plugging up was carried out according to the menu which showed the letters to be connected with each other. These wheel orders/menus were phoned through from Headquarters at Bletchley to the Eastcote Wren officer responsible for handing out the work to Wren operators.

Drums in place and plugging-up completed, the machine would be switched on, enabling the millions of permutations to begin.

We made our debut at midnight. Entering the room illuminated by fluorescent lighting was a new experience, like stepping from night into day. Then the ears took in the sound of bombes click-bonging away as rows of drums revolved and stopped, revolved and stopped. The nose also had its share of impressions – a particularly disagreeable smell of hot oil.

Each room, known as a bay and housing ten or twelve bombes, was named after a country in the Commonwealth. We were to be working in New Zealand. Margaret's bombe was called Wellington, June's Auckland and mine Gisborne.

Once we'd got the hang of it all the hours passed slowly since the work was tedious and monotonous. One girl decided this occupation was not for her. She complained to the Medical Officer that she was being plagued by nightmares in which long, thick leads wrapped themselves round her throat.

"Crafty so-and-so" I thought with envy when I heard she'd been transferred to non-secret clerical work.

Changing the wheel orders and plugging up for a new run every few hours gave one something to do and exercised the brain for a while, but with the machine switched on, plodding through its permutations, time dragged. Margaret sometimes stuck her head round the back of Gisborne to mock me with the words,

"Still changing wheel orders?" And later I might do the same to her.

Once she saved me mortification by waking me as I slept upright in my chair. Shortly before the end of the watch I'd been sitting there thinking about breakfast; the next minute there was Margaret shaking me.

"Wake up! First Officer is doing her rounds!"

A tiresome task with no end to it was to examine the spare drums for faults. The brushes inside must on no account touch each other since this could cause a short which could then result in a missed stop. If we found any erring brushes we separated them with a pair of fine tweezers. We took stubborn cases to the cubby-hole nearby where in a haze of cigarette smoke RAF technicians worked, maintaining the equipment we used. Whenever a stop was missed it was the technicians' job to come and inspect the bombe to find out what had gone wrong. Since mistakes did sometimes occur, each new menu and set of wheel orders had at least two bombes working on it. If Gisborne missed a 'good' stop it was unlikely that Wellington would too.

A stop occurred when the drums on a bombe ceased turning. The operator would then note on a piece of paper the letters opposite which the drums had come to a halt and pass this information to her checker. In the small room next door this Wren fed the combination of letters into her machine. If this confirmed that, for example, Y equalled A and then in due course that A equalled Y, and that perhaps W equalled W (termed a 'self stop') the odds were this was a 'good' stop and to be passed on to Headquarters.

During the early days, self stops were referred to as 'self steckers' but the German word was soon abandoned. If overheard by the enemy it could have alerted them to what was going on.

When a stop was good, the checker phoned the pairs of letters through to Bletchley. A little while later a shout of 'job up on Auckland!' might be heard and we'd know that another message was on its way to being cracked.

CHAPTER 4

On the evening of my eighteenth birthday Margaret and I rang home before going on night watch. We were shaken to hear that our younger brother Tom, a cadet at Pangbourne Nautical College, had been injured during a school rugger match and had developed osteomyelitis. Dismayed by this news and knowing that osteomyelitis could cripple or even cause death, it was in an anxious frame of mind that we went to work that night.

Half-way through the watch we stood round the four o'clock tea trolley (known for some reason as tea-boat) waiting for a hot drink. As was customary, everyone had left their bombes for this welcome diversion. Suddenly, the world appeared to be coming to an end. The building rocked, doors and windows were blown out of their frames and I became aware that my hair was standing on end: an odd sensation. Not fright but blast from an explosion had caused it.

"This is the end!" shot through my mind. But the noise subsided, the dust settled and our bombes trundled away, unaffected by all the excitement. No one seemed to know what to say or do next. Doubtless we all shared a feeling that such closeness to death ought to be acknowledged, but our remarks were either banal or silly. To hide the trembling of my hands I fetched a broom to sweep up broken glass. What a good thing, I reflected, that girls who'd normally have been sitting at their checking machines in front of windows covered only by black-out curtains had escaped the flying glass. As the bomb had timed its arrival for tea-boat time, no one had been hurt.

Coming off watch four hours later we hurried outside to view the crater gaping at us twenty-five yards from the huts in which we'd been working. (Somebody measured the distance). Small pieces of bomb lay scattered over the ploughed field. Using me as a screen an RAF officer took illicit photographs of the crater and detritus, while I perpetrated my own modest act of disobedience by picking up an object resembling a long nail with a leather collar at one end. We'd been told by our officers not to take any souvenirs, but this was asking too much. It was after all 'our' bomb.

Margaret and I then made for a telephone box in the Wrennery. Before telling Mother about the drama of the night we asked for news of Tom. Mother sounded cheerful.

"Tom is being treated by the Canadians!"

Across the road from the mental hospital was an annexe used by the LCC as an orphanage from the time of its construction early in the 19th century until the 1920s. The Canadian Army Medical Corps had taken over this annexe and also the hutted hospital put up in its grounds at the outbreak of war. When my father rang to tell him what had happened, the senior physician at once admitted Tom as a patient. Injections of a new drug called penicillin and not then readily available to civilians were to cure him completely. (Ten thousand Oxford Units of penicillin intramuscularly every three hours, my brother informed me years later).

As I lay in my bunk that morning I couldn't sleep: the smell of rotten eggs coming from my piece of doodlebug was overwhelming. There was nothing for it but to remove this treasure from the locker I shared with the occupant of the upper bunk and consign the object to the dustbin.

The Wrennery at Stanmore was handy for London, an exciting place where, you never knew, someone nice might turn up at one of the dance places we frequented. Lorry-drivers could be relied on to stop for us when we wanted to hitch-hike, although when in funds we'd catch a bus on the street outside the main gates. Sometimes we timed this badly and emerged from the Wrennery at six in time to see our bus approaching. As this was the hour at which the Ensign was lowered for the night we knew we should stand to attention and wait until the ceremony had been completed. This caused a nail-biting dilemma as to whether to behave in a respectful manner or make a dash for the bus.

The most favoured goal on Saturday afternoons was the Overseas Club in the West End. Admission was for officers only but if you were a woman it didn't matter what rank you were. We danced with Poles, Norwegians, members of the Fighting French and men from Commonwealth countries. We also danced with British men, of course. Wrens with American boyfriends patronised the Rainbow Club in Piccadilly; I was never asked out by an American but I didn't mind too much. To me they were more alien than the Poles or the French.

Emerging afterwards from the crowded, sweaty scene inside the Club, we liked to saunter along Regent Street to window-shop and agree on how pleasant it would be to have a sugar-daddy to buy us some of the luxuries still to be had. White silk scarves embroidered with the Royal Naval emblem were desirable, didn't need coupons and would have looked elegant when worn with the uniform winter overcoat. "Want must be your master" would no doubt have been our school matron's irritating admonishment.

In our cabin with its twenty or so double-decker bunks, Bing Crosby's voice provided a background to off-watch gossip, nail-polishing and getting ready to go out. Bing's voice was too saccharine for my taste but the Andrews Sisters were splendid. Infinitely preferable it was to have

"The boogy-woogy bugler boy of Company B" stuck on the brain than "I'm dreaming of a White Christmas".

The owner of the wind-up gramophone was able to boast that her American army officer threatened suicide if she didn't agree to be engaged. Impressive.

Thanks to our patronage of such places as the Hammersmith Palais our prowess on the dance floor improved. At school Margaret and I had had to learn ballroom dancing, every minute of which I'd hated: the compulsory wearing of shantung Sunday dresses, silk stockings and shoes with unfamiliar two inch heels; the clammy hands of a female partner and the clumsy attempt to master spin-turns and the one-two-three of a slow waltz. At the Palais, however, dancing became a joy and instead of a piano to provide the music we had Ted Heath and his Music.

And the matelots were especially good at making us feel like a Ginger Rogers to their Fred Astaire.

CHAPTER 5

As April progressed we knew that the war in Europe was not going to last much longer. On the 4th May 1945 the German army surrendered.

My mother used to enjoy describing the scene on the day when the 1914 War came to an end. On that 11th day of November 1918 strangers were running up to each other on the street exclaiming,

"Have you heard? The Armistice has been signed!"

Celebrations erupted throughout the country and little work was done. It wasn't like this in 1945, however. We had to restrain ourselves for four days before being given the go-ahead to celebrate Victory in Europe Day on the 8th May.

In the Wrennery at Stanmore we sat by the wireless in the fo'c'sle listening to Churchill's speech to the nation. Then we set off for London. We didn't have to wait long for a lift. An important-looking individual wearing a pin-striped suit pulled up in his Rolls to where we were standing. Margaret, June, a friend called Rosemary and I were then driven in considerable comfort all the way to Piccadilly Circus. There we got out of the car, thanked our chauffeur and merged with the crowds singing, dancing and rejoicing over the fact that in Europe at least the fighting had ceased.

Having sung "Land of hope and glory", or at least as many of the words as it knew, the crowd surged towards Buckingham Palace. After a long wait during which nothing had happened the four of us decided to head back for Stanmore. We wanted our tea.

The cheers we heard as we made for the tube suggested we'd missed by minutes the Royal Family's appearance on the Palace balcony.

Back at the Wrennery we found a V-sign of coloured lights strung on the walls of the tower outside our cabin. When darkness fell the sign would be visible for miles.

For the P5 Wrens one welcome consequence of peace was the fact that before the summer was out no more decoding work had to be done. Instead we were given the task of dismantling some of the Enigma equipment, the tiresome little drums in particular. We sat outside the huts in the sunshine, wearing our square-necked, short-sleeved matelot shirts, gossiping and not exerting ourselves too much. By means of screwdriver and pliers we took the drums to pieces, making them unidentifiable and suitable to be sent for scrap. Although the war had ended, Enigma was to remain a secret.

Then to our delight those of us who a year ago had volunteered to serve overseas were told their wish was soon to be granted, although to which part of the globe we were to be sent They were not saying. The war-time custom of keeping people in the dark about their ultimate destination until the last minute still prevailed. But the fact we were to be trained for several weeks in the docks at Portsmouth seemed to suggest we must be destined for a port.

June we discovered would be following on in a later draft. Although she had fallen in love with and was engaged to a Polish officer, she wanted to have this overseas experience before settling down into married life. To Margaret's and my disappointment and to June's, her draft for some reason never left the UK.

Based in Southsea, those of us who were destined to go overseas travelled each day to the docks at Pompey where we were lectured on such topics as how to calculate the capacity of storage tanks and how to order naval stores in triplicate.

After yawning our way through these sessions it was fun to stroll round Portsmouth, to be taken over HMS Victory and generally to enjoy summer by the sea. Sauntering along one morning in the sunshine, we stopped: a loudspeaker was announcing that on that day, the 6th of

August, an atomic bomb had been dropped on Hiroshima. The horrific scale of destruction wrought by this bomb was briefly described. Shame that it was our side who'd carried out this deed crept over me. The new kind of bomb sounded dreadfully evil.

Next we were transferred to Crosby Hall in Chelsea, an establishment in which Wrens about to depart overseas were prepared for their forthcoming adventure. There we were issued with the white tropical uniform: drill skirt, short-sleeved blouse, hat and lace-up canvas shoes. Anything new in the way of clothing was exciting, and especially pleasing were the bell-bottomed trousers and hand-knitted grey jerseys for the cool part of the sea voyage.

Then we set off on a week's embarkation leave but no sooner had Margaret and I arrived at our parents' holiday home on the North Norfolk coast than we received a telegram, delivered by the Wells policeman on his bike. We must return to Crosby Hall at once.

In a state of excitement and with no regrets at having to cut the holiday short we travelled back to Chelsea where we learnt that our destination was to be Ceylon.

Before we'd had time to pass this information on to our families, let alone any spies, we were down in Southampton; with kitbag in one hand and suitcase in the other we boarded the "Athlone Castle".

Embarking through an opening onto a lower deck I was surprised to find myself walking across coloured lino, the pre-war version of vinyl floor covering, while white-jacketed stewards hovered, waiting to show us to our cabins. Since this was a troop ship I'd imagined her decks would be of bare planks and although not sailing before the mast exactly, as ratings we'd naturally be travelling under spartan conditions. For the troops this was certainly so: we could see as we went on board hundreds of hammocks with little space between each slung from the low deckhead. The privileged Wrens, however, were escorted to a higher deck where until 1939 cabin-class passengers had been accommodated. These single-berth cabins now contained double-decker bunks.

The first morning at sea Margaret and I were surprised but pleased to be woken by a steward bearing a tray of tea. When he learnt that I didn't like tea, the steward brought me instant coffee instead.

Thus began an ocean voyage made even more thrilling by the fact that men on board outnumbered women by a hundred to one. Not one of us need lack a choice of male partners for the dances, deck games, films and sessions of housey-housey. Although at home we'd played Lotto I was unfamiliar with this grown-up version and found such calls as "66 – clicketyclick", "seven and six – was she worth it?" to be tremendously witty.

One morning as the white uniforms of the crew sparkled in the sunshine, we were given a keep-fit class on the boat deck by a Wren officer. Wearing shorts, blouses and gym shoes we soon attracted an audience of young men and when our activities came to an end we mingled with them. I was greatly taken with a grey-eyed sub-lieutenant, sturdily built, about my own height and with perfect teeth. His name was Tony and we arranged to go to the cinema together that evening.

Even without the young men, the voyage would have been idyllic because of the food. The ship had victualled in South Africa and we couldn't remember having eaten so well.

To complete our sense of well-being the sun shone warmly in a cloudless blue sky once we were past Gibraltar. This was the life and we were to have it all the way to Ceylon.

At the next stop, Malta, however, disappointing news was conveyed to us. A signal from the Admiralty to First Officer informed her that the draft of Wrens for Ceylon had been cancelled: we must disembark at Port Said and await passage back to the UK. No explanation was given to us for this change of plan. We assumed the Admiralty had belatedly decided it would be a waste of taxpayers' money to send us such a long way to do clerical work that could surely by undertaken by local people. Never mind, we thought. We had had an exhilarating time in this former cruise liner and at least we had the voyage home to look forward to.

CHAPTER 6

Addresses exchanged with the young men continuing the voyage without us, we disembarked at Port Said. From there we were driven for a couple of hours in canvas-topped lorries to HMS Phoenix, a Fleet Air Arm repair base. Covering a large expanse of desert in the vicinity of the Great Bitter Lakes and surrounded by a high wire fence, HMS Phoenix was also used as a transit camp for service personnel. The base contained hangars, workshops, quarters for officers, ratings and Italian prisoners-of-war, a small stone church, a theatre and acres of asphalt smelling of hot oil: an agreeable smell quite different from the one given off by the Enigma machines.

How long we could expect to be in Egypt no one knew, but to keep us occupied we were all assigned tasks about the base. Margaret spent her working hours processing invoices while I spent mine typing letters for a sub-lieutenant in charge of one of the workshops. If somewhat boring, the days were relaxed, punctuated at frequent intervals by the consumption of dark brown tea accompanied by buns filled with sweet, gritty cream made from peanuts. This was brought to us by a local boy who squatted down in his djellabah to hand out the mugs, not minding in the least the dreadful Arabic practised on him by the ratings.

Courteous young Sudanese wearing Persil-white djellabahs and red fezes waited on us in the mess. Patiently at tea-time they responded not once but several times to our cries of,

"Abdul! More butter, please!"

Although from out of a tin the butter was a luxury we couldn't get enough of. Less appealing was the white bread speckled with dead weevils. Holding up a slice to the light we'd pick out the black bits before applying butter and jam onto what by this time resembled a lace mat.

One of these amiable servants, a little older than the rest and evidently their foreman, came into the fo'c'sle one evening as I was writing a letter to my father. He asked me what my father did and we talked about our families for a while. I longed for him to go on speaking as his voice had a gentle, caressing quality that brought me out in gooseflesh.

Invitations from Messes both inside and outside HMS Phoenix appeared on the Wren notice board. We could take our pick; those from the officers based in the camp we always accepted since for their dances they could boast a live orchestra whose musicians were German prisoners-of-war. We'd seen their camp stretching across the desert, the turned-up sides of the tents revealing a neatness of bedding and possessions to gladden the heart of any school matron.

"Lili Marlene" was everyone's favourite and we all joined in with the words sung in English with great feeling by the German vocalist.

If there was no dance to go to there'd usually be a film or a concert by touring members of Ensa (Entertainments National Service Association). One evening a soprano of substantial proportions began her performance with the song "I'm forever blowing bubbles"; the inappropriateness of this choice for a woman her size provoked spontaneous laughter from the audience, but nobody could have blamed the men for reacting as they did. Mortification on the singer's behalf and her obvious affront rendered the occasion acutely painful for many of us.

Egyptians came into HMS Phoenix every day from nearby villages to carry out various menial tasks. These included the emptying of our thunder-boxes as the Elsan-type lavatories were known. One Sunday morning in October the cleaners arrived an hour too soon, knowing nothing about clocks having gone back an hour, and through the aperture provided in the outside wall of the hut snatched the bucket from under the seat while I was reading a letter from home. I sat for several minutes, giggling like a maniac.

I blush to recall we learnt to refer to these workers as wogs, following the example of naval personnel in the camp. It wasn't until our eventual arrival in Ceylon that I began to feel uneasy about the use of such words and the lack of respect, to say the least, they conveyed.

One starlit evening I was invited to the camp cinema by the Master at Arms, or Jaunty as he was known in the Navy. A man over six feet in height, he had the job of maintaining discipline in the camp. When the film was over we walked across the sand towards the Wrennery, passing within a few yards of a small building with bars on the windows. From inside came whacking noises, followed by yelps.

"What on earth's going on in there?"

"Some wog's been caught stealing. They're giving him six of the best. A beating's the only thing they understand."

A few days later the Jaunty asked me to go along to one of the Wren cabins to identify formally a pair of black silk stockings as being the property of a Wren. The stockings had been discovered wrapped round the waist of a worker as he prepared to leave the camp at the day's end. When we arrived at the cabin, the man, forlorn in his ragged djellabah, stood with head hanging, a military police on either side of him.

When shown the stockings I had to agree that they must have belonged to a Wren but I ventured to point out that since both stockings were laddered they would undoubtedly have been thrown in the waste paper bin. The unfairness of the police who had made up their minds to treat this incident as theft, taking no notice of my remark, upset me far more than the whacking I'd heard.

For a brief period I enjoyed the attentions of the Surgeon-Commander based on the camp. Owning a small green sports car he took me one evening to the French Club in nearby Ismailia, a pleasant small town with its trees, shrubs and flowers. As we drove through the dark our headlights picked out a camel stalking along on the other side of the high fence, a rifle-bearing Arab on its back. Perhaps the man was simply going home to his supper but I preferred to imagine he was on his way to some assignation of significance in the Sinai desert.

The outing to Ismailia was not a success: I had no small talk and could think of nothing to say. In desperation and believing a doctor could only be interested in medical matters, I asked him what a coronary thrombosis was. He explained carefully, but after that evening there were no more outings for me in the nice little car.

A few weeks into our Egyptian experience some other Wrens, Margaret and I volunteered to sell Remembrance Day poppies. She and I took the task seriously, doing brisk business in parts of the camp hitherto unfrequented by Wrens. We found ourselves in a roomy shed where several Italian prisoners-of-war were at work. About to make a satisfactory sale to the men in their brown uniform, we were interrupted by a Petty Officer. With heavy tact he suggested,

"I don't think these chaps are interested in buying poppies."

They were, of course, and as PO escorted us out the Italians looked as disappointed as Margaret and I felt.

Outings were arranged for us to Suez, Port Said and Cairo. At Port Said's Simon Artz Store the Stewart sisters bought themselves white sling-back shoes, the epitome of elegance in their view. Then four of us ventured into a small, dark shop displaying silver filigree jewellery. As we looked and pondered, the shop owner courteously offered us coffee.

"Oh, no, thank you!"

"I expect you're afraid it will be drugged," he suggested, having correctly read the reason for our refusal.

He knew a thing or two about the sort of warnings given to nice English girls by their mothers. Sadly, none of us found anything we liked enough to buy.

A trip to Cairo some weeks later involved an overnight stay and an opportunity either to see the pyramids and sphinx or to spend an hour or two shopping in the city. The pyramids can wait, Margaret and I decided. Antiquities were fascinating, of course, but who knew when we'd next get the opportunity of going into shops where all sorts of goods could be found and for which you needed no coupons? Therefore, while the others went off to take in some culture, my sister and I were dropped off in the centre of Cairo where once again we found ourselves looking at shoes. The Egyptian who ran the shop appeared to enjoy the selling as much as we did the buying. My choice was a pair of high-heeled, peep-toe, soft tan leather shoes, tremendously glamorous. By lightly caressing my ankle with both hands as he fitted the shoes the man managed to persuade me they were a good fit even though they weren't. (A size too small, they were only worn once, but in due course a Wren with smaller feet was pleased to buy them from me for ten shillings.)

While paying for our purchases we became aware of the wail of sirens from approaching cars. Everyone was hustled outside onto the pavement. And to polite rather than enthusiastic clapping a red convertible, escorted by police cars and large enough for a football team, swept past, the back seat occupied by a fat man wearing a fez and dark glasses.

Philistines we may have been in having chosen to shop rather than visit two of the Wonders of the World but at least we could boast that we'd seen King Farouk.

CHAPTER 7

The stars over Egypt appeared closer and more brilliant than any we'd seen over England and by the third week in December it was easy to imagine a particularly large one hovering over a village not far away.

On Christmas Eve with these stars glittering overhead a group of men and girls went round the camp carol-singing, ending up outside the ratings' mess. The shouts, laughter and singing booming out from within drowned any sounds we were making. The ratings showed no interest in our singing, not only because they'd drunk a lot but undoubtedly because our conductor made us sing "While shepherds watched..." to the tune of "Ilkley Moor..." The traditional tune might have brought some of them outside for a proper listen.

At half-past-eleven we walked across the moonlit sand for midnight communion in the little stone church. A group of Wrens came in at the last minute, evidently straight from a party. Having been instructed at confirmation classes three years previously that we must attend communion in a thoughtful, certainly sober, frame of mind, I was shocked by these late-comers in their long dresses. Perhaps, though, a Wren I spoke to afterwards was right: Our Lord would rather we turn up than stay away.

Diversion in the form of camel and donkey rides was provided for us on Boxing Day. Diminutive creatures, the donkeys looked well cared-for with glossy coats and dainty hooves. My feet touched the ground as I sat on my beast but in spite of his small stature he couldn't be bent to my will. He trotted with determination towards the perimeter fence – a long way off. Eventually his owner caught up with us and led donkey and rider back to the others.

Riding a camel provided an interesting experience also. Difficult though it was to remain in the saddle when the animal lurched to its feet from a crouching position – tight uniform skirt not helping – once up there and on the move the rocking gait became acceptable. That my best nylons had become laddered was a fair price to pay for being able to enjoy this unusually lofty view of the camp.

Accustomed though we were to a steady flow of invitations, the evening ahead was to be special. It was New Year's Eve and we were off to Port Said. The Wrens from HMS Phoenix had been invited to a dance taking place in one of the port's principal hotels and our hosts were to be officers from the three services.

With cases packed for an overnight stay in the YWCA we set off on the desert drive as shadows began to lengthen over the sand in front of our cabin. At the sight of all these girls in grey pullovers and bell-bottomed trousers, sitting or standing in canvas-topped lorries, some labourers working on the road turned somersalts shouting "Aywah!" as they did so. Whether they were expressing admiration or derision we couldn't tell.

Darkness had fallen by the time we reached our destination and our immediate need after booking in was to remove a thick coating of dust from hands, faces and necks.

During our last visit home Mother had given both of us one of her evening dresses. Margaret's, of bronze taffeta, was roomier than it need have been but we both appreciated the way it rustled. Mine, also of taffeta, was covered in lace the colour of pink marshmallows. To complete its Doris Day appearance it sported a Peter Pan collar and small buttons all the way up to the neck. Sexy they certainly weren't, but never mind, the dresses were floor-length and we felt important in them.

Delivered to the hotel in a small bus, we were drawn towards the action by the sound of a dance band. In the foyer stood a group of young men in their best uniforms waiting to greet the Wrens who in no time were quick-stepping and spin-turning on the sprung floor.

During a band-break Margaret and I headed for the Ladies to renew powder and lipstick. A resumption of the music then inspired us to jitterbug until laughter threatened to spoil our make-up. Returning to the dance, my sister waltzed off with a young man in khaki and I with a naval officer. Two-and-a-half rings on his cuff denoted the rank of Lieutenant commander. A snob over pecking orders, I was gratified to be partnered by a Lt Cdr RN as opposed to Lt Cdr RNVR. That he was 'permanent' navy enhanced his standing.

While we danced Nicholas told me he was serving in HMS Howe – a battleship, no less! And as well as status he possessed blue-grey eyes, a gentle manner and the ability to dance in time. During a slow waltz we sat at the bar, exchanging biographical details while sipping from his pigskin flask. The barman didn't mind. My companion had already consumed quite a bit I could tell, but it didn't show all that much.

Presently Nicholas suggested we find a room with an open fire. Wizard idea! Unbelievably naive at the age of nineteen even by 1945 standards I fell in with the plan. Upstairs corridors stretched both ways from a large landing. Nicholas opened a door. Unsurprisingly no sitting-room with fireplace was revealed. Peering over his shoulder I saw an unmade bed. (How slovenly, I clucked inwardly.) Then:

"But these are all bedrooms!"

Ignoring this remark and grabbing me by the hand he did his best to pull me over the threshold. Shocked but wishing to demonstrate sophistication I admonished him in Noel Cowardish tones:

"I don't think your intentions are strictly honourable."

"You're damned right, darling. They're not."

But the fact that his alcoholic intake over the past hours had been much greater than mine gave him a handicap; it wasn't long before I was able to yank him back to the respectable side of the door. Accepting defeat without rancour Nicholas led the way back down the stairs.

I slunk down after him, mortified to think that the world must be jumping to conclusions as to where we'd been. But if anyone had noticed our return from bedroom territory the ballroom was at that moment crowded with couples hugging, kissing and singing 'Auld Lang

Syne'. 1946 had arrived. The goings-on of the muggins in the pink dress interested no one.

With the last waltz reaching its sentimental conclusion Nicholas summoned a horse-drawn gharri into which we both climbed. Leaning back against ancient leather upholstery smelling strongly of horse, I looked forward to the moment when I could flop onto my bed, take off my shoes... I froze: Nicholas was ordering the driver to take us to the beach.

The beach! In Port Said! This could be the prelude to a fate worse than death hinted at but never quite spelt out by Mother. I shouted to the driver

"No! To the YWCA!"

"To the beach!"

The horse plodded along, the hunched-up figure of the driver displaying no interest in either of us. Now I was alarmed. As an Arab the driver would surely obey Nicholas rather than me. Must I jump out and run for it?

Then the gharri came to a halt and there was the lovely sight of the hostel. Resisting an urge to hug the driver I bolted from the vehicle and waved farewell to Nicholas from the sanctuary of the YWCA.

The next morning on an upstairs balcony while we waited to set off on the long drive back to HMS Phoenix I gazed at the harbour visible in the distance. A grey ship with the unmistakable lines of a battleship was heading slowly for the Mediterranean bearing my wicked commander with her. I felt sad, though. In some ways he had reminded me of my film star idol, the late Leslie Howard.

CHAPTER 8

Splendid news arrived for us in the New Year: the draft to Ceylon had been reinstated, the Admiralty having come to the conclusion we'd be useful out there after all.

On a cold but sparkling day in January, with cases and kitbags packed and goodbyes said to various young men, we set off in our old friends the 3-ton lorries for the drive to Port Said. There we boarded an elderly ship named the "Alcantara". This vessel we found to be full of Dutch troops and medical personnel en route to the fighting in Java. Also aboard was a draft of Dutch Wrens.

We liked these people, especially the young doctors, but were less interested in our Dutch counterparts. These girls envied us our cool canvas shoes, trying without much success to persuade some of us to exchange them for the ones with which they'd been issued – good-quality buckskin, guaranteed to make the feet hot.

To help pass the time as the ship progressed through the Suez Canal and into the long slog of the Red Sea the Dutch soldiers held concerts for their own amusement down in the crowded lower decks. They sang in harmony in such a way that even "You are my sunshine" sounded beautiful. The temperature rose fiercely in the Red Sea and for two nights the heat in our cabins was unendurable. We were therefore given permission to collect up our bedding and sleep under the stars. Once inside the Arabian Sea, however, it became merely hot again, encouraging us to spend pleasant hours lolling about in the sunshine with our doctor friends.

The idyll came to an end when we disembarked at Colombo leaving the Dutch to continue their journey to Java.

During the voyage First Officer had allowed each of us to choose whether we'd stay in Colombo or continue on to Trincomalee on the other side of the island. Those who plumped for Colombo included my sister.

My mind was still on my Sub-Lieutenant from the Athlone Castle and I knew from the letters he'd written to me while we were in Egypt that he was by this time stationed in Trincomalee. I took it for granted he was eagerly awaiting my arrival. I therefore asked to be part of the Trincomalee contingent.

Our numbers having been divided into two groups to everyone's satisfaction, Margaret and I said goodbye to each other for the first time in our lives. While she and her party set off for Hatton Court, the Wrennery in Colombo, the rest of us were taken to the railway station where we caught the train for Trincomalee.

All day the train chugged through countryside whose greenness dazzled after the greys and yellows of Egypt. During one of the stops, when local people surged into and out of the packed, unreserved carriages, a fruit vendor stood beneath our window offering a basket of pineapples. I bought one of these beauties and with the help of a pen-knife and a handkerchief to catch the drips I proceeded to eat the whole fruit by myself. My greed was punished when the inside of my mouth started to feel as though it had been chewing stinging nettles.

Built some distance from the town and dockyard the Wrennery in

Trincomalee stood inside a stockaded compound with matelots guarding the main gate. The living quarters were housed in low buildings referred to as bandas. Overhanging thatched roofs provided insulation against the rays of the sun and as we stepped inside to claim our bunks we experienced not coolness exactly but refuge from the heat. The wooden shutters over unglazed windows stayed open except when the monsoon rains roared down. At mealtimes we were waited on by gentle brown-skinned men wearing white shirts and long wrap-over skirts.

Although well supplied with trees the compound was kept clear of any other greenery; the hard-baked earth was swept daily, thus depriving snakes and creepy-crawlies of hiding places. Lizards and gheckos looked down at us from the rafters and we learnt to respect them for their ability to catch mosquitoes. The trees overlooking our bandas were home to small furry tree-rats resembling chipmunks, disappointingly timid.

Other tree-dwellers we were to see during outings into the countryside were gibbons resembling small boys in grey-blue velvet suits. Cuddly to look at they could apparently turn nasty if anyone came within touching distance.

From Mondays to Fridays we worked in the dockyard offices. I sat behind a typewriter in a Naval Stores Department run by two civil servants from the UK and assisted by Tamils and Sinhalese. Two of these, Devendra and Rajalingum, were unfailingly polite and helpful, coming to my rescue one day when I jumped up in horror having found in my desk drawer a spider resembling jointed grey sticks. Judging from Devendra's reaction as he snatched the drawer out and stamped on the creature I realised it was not a species they wished to tangle with. That it had survived in the office at all was surprising because each week a man with a tank on his back sprayed everything, us included, with a suffocating cloud of DDT. (It seemed to occur to no one that it might be healthier for us to wait outside).

Our officers warned us never to go out alone after dark. In their desire for independence the people of Ceylon were becoming less and less warm towards the British. Ugly incidents were occurring more frequently in Colombo than in Trincomalee, however; a Wren had seen her boy-friend fatally stabbed as they walked along a quiet road.

The only intimation of anti-British feeling I ever received was when a friend had taken me one evening to see "Brief Encounter" at the town cinema. Emerging onto the street afterwards with a lump in my throat I was given an unmistakable message when a fist landed hard on my diaphragm. It hurt but did no harm and there seemed little point in mentioning it to my escort. Even if he'd wanted to do something about it in such a crowd it was impossible to see who had delivered the blow.

That some of the people disliked us intensely didn't surprise me. I'd witnessed the offensive way in which a British NCO had shouted at a Sinhalese sitting minding his own business, addressing him as "Johnny!" and demanding that he approach for some reason or other. To this particular sergeant, and he was not alone, all these brown men were "Johnny" and should be prepared to jump to his command.

During the hours of daylight it was safe to go alone to the pettah, as the market was called, either to have a dress made by one of the many skilled tailors or to wander through stalls of handmade goods and wonder which of these to take home as presents for the family when the time came. The occasional white bullock meandering down the street and getting in everyone's way had to be avoided. This sacred animal was allowed to do as it pleased.

The Wrens had their own private jetty from which to swim at weekends although the heat of the sun made it impossible for me at least to laze about for long. Sooner or later the lure of my bunk for an afternoon zizz became irresistible. But as soon as I lay down I became drenched in sweat; there was nothing for it but to retreat outside to a patch of shade.

CHAPTER 9

Having recovered from mortification over the fact that soon after my arrival in Trinco Tony had became enamoured of an attractive nurse, I was being taken out by a different Sub-Lieutenant whose job was to look after three small motor minesweepers moored in the harbour. Conversation between him and me was heavy-going since we had little in common. But for a while I enjoyed being collected in his motor cutter for the short journey to the minesweeper whose diminutive wardroom he had all to himself. There we drank port and played Monopoly while the Andrews Sisters belted out "Rum and coca-cola!" on the gramophone. This record had been banned in the States because of the rude things it said about the 'Yankee dollar' earned by certain ladies in Trinidad. Listening to it while drinking port in the afternoon seemed the height of sophistication.

One afternoon my friend headed the long cutter towards a rusty iron buoy anchored in a quiet part of the harbour where we'd have a swim before tea. Obedient to his instructions, I stood in the bow with a line in my hand and at the moment of impact with the side of the buoy I leapt onto its rough surface, clinging on while it rocked to and fro. Once it had calmed down, and feeling pleased with myself for not having fallen off, I was able to fasten the line to a metal ring. We then had our swim.

Another pastime to divert three of us for a week or two was target shooting. Joy, Elaine and I accepted an invitation to be taught this skill by members of the Royal Marine Sergeants' Mess. We'd go along on Saturday afternoons to lie on our stomachs and shoot with .22 rifles at stationary targets. Once when the lesson was over my instructor let me fire his .45 revolver and it was all I could do to pull the trigger of the heavy weapon, let alone hit a tree standing six feet away. He explained how difficult it was even for experienced people to be accurate with a revolver, especially when the target was moving, in spite of evidence to the contrary depicted in cowboy films. Then we all sat drinking beer on the Mess verandah, to be joined after a while by the sergeants' pet mongoose. He also liked his beer, clasping the rim of the mug with his paws as he drank.

When these shooting lessons came to an end our sergeant friends took several of us on a long drive to see the ruins of Anuradhapura, site of Ceylon's first capital that dated back to the 4th century BC. Having removed our shoes before entering one of the sacred Bhuddist precincts, we hopped from one tuft of grass to another to avoid being scorched by the heat of the stone paving. With the ruins inspected and marvelled at we then proceeded to a shady spot for a picnic. By this time we needed to spend a penny but before we disappeared behind the bushes our escorts searched the undergrowth with drawn revolvers to make sure no snakes lurked.

Twice I took a week-end pass to visit Margaret in Colombo and once she visited me. The humid heat of Colombo was more oppressive than that of Trinco and yet in the design of the prefabricated huts put up for the Wrens no concessions to the climate had been made: not even large ceiling fans to provide a gentle stirring of the air over the girls' bunks.

There could be other disadvantages, too. Margaret told me that one day upon opening an infrequently-used drawer beside her bed she'd been greeted by a horrid sight: amongst her winter clothes nestled a family of baby rats.

A gardener raking flower-beds in the compound took the drawer outside but, as a Bhuddist, wouldn't harm the rats. He merely tipped them out into the grass. No doubt the mother rat found them later and took them to another hide-out.

The highlight of my second Colombo visit was to be invited out to dinner by Eric, a 23-year-old-naval officer. He wearing white mess jacket, cummerbund and black trousers and I my long pink dress, the two of us ate well in the Galle Face Hotel, washing it all down with a bottle of four star brandy he'd bought in the mess for a small sum. Inexpensive spirits and liqueurs were freely available to officers from the Services and as their guests we enjoyed trying all kinds of alcoholic drinks. Gin and lime by then had its rivals.

Dinner over we managed to walk back to the car in a fairly straight line for the drive to the beach. Moonlight swims were considered by the Wrens and their boyfriends to be the thing to do and I was ready to give it a go.

Eric parked his car under a tree and then modestly withdrew to change into his trunks, leaving me to struggle into my bathing suit in the back of the car. Together we then approached the water.

No sooner did I plunge into the breakers thundering in from the Indian Ocean than it became clear we'd chosen a dangerous spot for this romantic dip. A wave at least twice my height crashed down, hurling me to my knees; with water and small pebbles crashing about me, I managed to struggle to my feet and clawed my way back to the dry sand. There, shivering inside a towel, I was joined by my equally battered companion. We cuddled up together, glad of each other's warmth.

Then I happened to look up. Silhouetted against the night sky along the top of the cliff was a row of heads all turned in our direction. Their owners were waiting to see what we'd get up to next. The sight of the silent spectators coupled with the chill coming off the sea, dictated an immediate withdrawal from the beach and for me a return to the Wrennery. Although this wasn't the way in which he'd intended the evening to end, Eric was no more keen than I to provide entertaimnent for the row of heads, and so it was back to town and our respective beds.

The following day I awoke to my first hangover. The pain in my head was unbelievable but with the help of some Veganin Margaret found, I'd recovered sufficiently to go sailing in the afternoon. Sunglasses were not much in evidence in those days and I developed a vicious migraine from the glare reflected from the water of the harbour. Still suffering I was driven that evening by Eric to catch my train. He took me to the Rail Traffic Officer whose responsibility it was to find me a seat. This he did. Marching up to a carriage crowded with Sinhalese soldiers he flung open the door.

"Out!" he bellowed.

Obediently the young men picked up their belongings and filed onto the platform, all hope of finding seats now gone.

Cringeing with embarrassment over the soldiers' treatment but desperate to lie down and shut my eyes I climbed into the carriage. The RTO then locked the door to ensure I had the compartment to myself for the entire journey. How I was released at the other end I can't remember but by the time we reached Trincomalee my headache had gone.

Halfway through their Ceylon experience the Wrens in Colombo and Trinco were sent up-country on leave. Margaret and her friends took a train that wound its way up from Colombo into the hills, while we travelled from the eastern side of the island in a Naval bus.

Leaving the coast the road climbed steadily. And although at sea level I hadn't been aware of a damp film covering my skin, I realised with pleasure when we reached an altitude of a few thousand feet that for the first time for months my skin felt cool and dry.

At 4,000 feet we reached Nuwara Eliya, literally in the clouds: the air cold, visibility nil. With a brief stop to eat sandwiches and use a hotel lavatory we continued our journey, the ascent becoming ever more steep. Every few yards I shut my eyes while the bus navigated a sharp bend.

For some of us the journey ended in a daze of car-sickness. Recovery was swift, however, when we got off the bus and walked into the leave centre at Diyatalawa, a sort of holiday camp spread over undulating countryside. This was tea-plantation country, with hills and valleys on all sides. The air was fresh and stimulating and smelt of flowers and woodsmoke.

We discovered the Wrens weren't the only ones on leave in this place. On our first evening at a dance held in the camp we met young officers from the army and navy. After a thoroughly satisfying evening we were invited to join some of them next day for a picnic.

With food and beer on board we drove in a lorry to the perfect spot. There were trees for shade, large rocks to sit on and a pool at the foot of a small waterfall. Although most of us changed into bathing suits only the hardy ventured into bitterly cold water. I certainly had no intention of inflicting a nasty shock on my system but was glad of an excuse to wear for the first time a two-piece bathing suit made for me by a local tailor.

"You look cool" remarked a young man reclining on the ground in white shorts and shirt.

Pleased though I was by his obvious approval, I was also shy, clutching my bath towel against me.

He was attractive, and I was glad to sit next to him while we ate our lunch. When I commented on the phenomenon of a girl I didn't consider nearly as pretty as I was sitting on a rock holding court, the circle of young-men clearly enjoying her company and conversation, he observed,

"They like her because she is unself-conscious. She puts them at their ease."

(In the Wrens looks mattered, and on joining up I'd been told more than once that I was pretty. Such comments had never been made to me before and they went to my head. That there was more to being attractive than mere prettiness took a long time to sink in. Meanwhile, I enjoyed the erroneous belief that I was a cross between Rita Hayworth and Helen of Troy.)

During our leave we were taken to a communion service in a small white-washed church set down on a hillside overlooking tea plantations. Inside the building a thick beam divided the chancel from the nave. At a moment when we were all on our knees a movement from above distracted me from the prayers: a ginger cat appeared at one end of the beam, then stalked across to the other side, looking down at us with interest as he did so and in no hurry to complete his journey.

Emerging from the cool, dim interior and blinking for a moment in the sun, Margaret and I were joined by a family of Sinhalese in their European-style Sunday best walking down the path to their parked car.

"A beautiful service!" remarked the father, a smile lighting up his dark features.

Apart from the dull sermon it had indeed been a beautiful service.

A few days later we had to pack and leave, to swelter at sea level for a few more months.

CHAPTER 10

'Officers' Popsies' was how we were referred to by the ratings stationed in Trinco. Officers were popular as boyfriends: no doubt they seemed more glamorous. (Glamour mattered too). They certainly had more money, enjoyed easier access to private transport and their Club was posher than the one provided for the Other Ranks. Hardly surprising therefore that officers had an edge on the less-favoured NCOs and ratings.

My conscience was clear: I'd shared my spare time with a succession of young men, commissioned and non-commissioned, never keeping any particular boyfriend for long.

Although the Combined Services Club for the other ranks may have lacked the superior ambience of the Officers' Club, once a week it offered a magnificent opportunity for us to dance in serious fashion to a live band. Three of us took advantage of this, going along every Wednesday evening to dance non-stop for two or three hours. Most of the men there had to dance with each other since there were few women to go round. As we fox-trotted, quick-stepped, waltzed or tangoed there was little conversation. When the music paused different young men would come up to whisk us away into the next dance.

The evening flew until the moment when the band struck up its signature tune "There's a new world over the skyline", signalling far too early the time to go home to bed.

A special treat laid on for the Wrens one Saturday in March was to spend a day at sea. Early in the morning we were taken in small boats to the side of HMS Petard, a destroyer anchored in the harbour.

Once aboard we were escorted to the quarters of our hosts for the day: wardroom for the Wren officers, Chief Petty Officers' mess for the Wren ratings.

For those of us who weren't fussy about getting dirty a tour of the ship included the opportunity to climb up to the masthead. Stopping short of the top – too high for me – I gazed at the sparkling waters of the Indian Ocean, its surface empty except for us. By the time I descended to the deck my hands were black and greasy. Cleaning off the worst with a piece of rag, I followed the others to the CPOs' mess.

The Chiefs and Petty Officers showed no signs of regarding us as popsies of any kind but the morning having started so early tended to drag. When the hour for lunch finally arrived we were all offered a tot of rum.

It was customary in the Royal Navy for those below officer rank who'd reached the age of eighteen to be given a daily tot – an eighth of a pint – and we'd each be taking someone's ration for the day. There were however only two takers and the rum was supposed to be consumed in one gulp. Elaine drank hers in several sips, while, show- off Stewart downed hers in two gulps. The effect of this sudden intake of strong drink was immediate: a pleasing anaesthetic spreading to all limbs. Nevertheless I managed to eat most of my lunch before being overwhelmed by drowsiness at the pudding stage. One of the CPOs slung his hammock, deep, narrow and made of canvas. Hoisting myself into it I fell asleep.

By the time I woke from a blissful respite from the necessity to make conversation, HMS Petard was nearing Trincomalee harbour.

Before descending to the waiting small boats, we thanked our hosts for looking after us all day and arranged to meet them in Trinco for a meal of fresh prawns later in the week. Back in the Wrennery I sat on my bunk and polished the present given to me by the owner of the hammock: a silver bo'sun's pipe on which with the point of his penknife he'd inscribed "HMS Petard, March 1946".

As the months passed, the round of social events lost its savour. Before setting off from Crosby Hall we'd been told it was our duty to go out with men who'd been away from home for a long time, a duty that ought not to present any hardship. But apart from the Wednesday evening dance sessions and Tuesday gramophone concerts given from a vehicle known as the 'Rediffusion Van', my keenest enjoyment had come to be from climbing into bed at night with a library book and bottle of cold beer. The world outside the mosquito net would then cease to exist.

September arrived and with it the news that our stay in Ceylon was to end. The Colombo Wrens had already left. Some of the girls were desolate, especially those leaving boyfriends behind. I could hardly wait to go home.

In October we piled with our luggage into lorries to be driven to the station where we'd take the train across to Colombo and our awaiting ship. Hunched over a small case containing precious souvenirs, I sat at the back of the lorry, impatient for us all to get going and fearful that something might happen at the last minute to stop us. Near me a Wren wept bitterly. She'd just been informed by the young man to whom she thought she'd been engaged that it had been fun knowing her but that this was goodbye.

Although enjoyable enough the voyage home in the "Otranto" had little of the excitement of the outward journey. To prepare us for the shock of the austerity conditions still prevailing in Britain we were given a demonstration of the weekly rations on which civilians subsisted: 2 ounces of butter and 2 of margarine, 2 ounces respectively of cheese, bacon and tea, 4 ounces of meat, and so on. We were not greatly bothered. We were on our way home.

Disembarking at Southampton we took a train to Southsea. There in a Wrennery already familiar from the previous year I was reunited with my sister. Dumping my stuff in the cabin allotted to us I joined her in a small room where Second Officer was giving a gramophone concert. The monotonous rhythm of Litoff's Concerto will forever remind me of that evening in October 1946 and the excitement of seeing Margaret again.

Two or three weeks were disposed of while we all waited for demob papers to come through. Having been eager at the age of 17 to join the Wrens, at the age of 19 I could hardly wait to get out. Even saluting officers and calling them Ma'am had come to seem anachronistic .

A branch of the service known as Educational and Vocational Training gave those who asked for it advice on what to do next in civilian life. Girls like my sister who'd acquired Higher School Certificate before joining up were encouraged to aim for college or university. They'd be eligible for a government grant, something new in those days. For me the prospect of taking up from where I'd thankfully left off at the age of 16 lacked charm. In any case, the nine months I'd spent at St James's Secretarial College for Gentlewomen qualified me for a job as secretary.

However, from somewhere had come the conviction that I must do my bit for mankind and as a secretary I didn't think I'd be doing it. I decided to train to be a nurse. I liked the thought of starting something from scratch and enjoyed the approbation of a young red-headed Wren officer who urged,

"Don't let anyone put you off!"

Her remark reinforced my feeling that nursing was for me.

At last one autumn day Margaret and I were given demob papers, rail vouchers and, most exciting of all, a clothing grant of £20. Margaret set off to stay with friends while I, before catching the train for Scotland, had a lovely time shopping. I spent the precious money on a Viyella blouse, white embroidered Austrian cardigan and an apple-green woollen dress I never really liked.

Part II

ROYAL INFIRMARY EDINGBURGH

1948–1950

CHAPTER 1

My father beamed when I told him of my plan; and as a graduate of that city's University he felt that the Edinburgh Royal Infirmary was the only school of nursing to be considered. I therefore wrote a letter of application to the matron, or Lady Superintendent of Nurses as she was known.

By the time I received a date for interview I'd decided to give myself a year off but I was invited to attend anyway. The tall, unsmiling woman in dark blue silky uniform dress and frilled cap proposed that I should join the December 1st 1947 intake of probationers. So forbidding did I find her that I hadn't the nerve to point out this would put paid to any ideas of celebrating my 21st birthday on the 17th.

1947 whizzed past in my parents' new home on the shores of Loch Awe. I had sailing lessons from my father, learnt Scottish country dancing, whist and badminton in the village hall and joined the Women's Rural Institute. During August when the sun bathed the Highlands in glorious technicolor for four whole weeks, I became engaged to a District Officer on leave from Tanganyika and disengaged a week later.

He and I met three times, twice on a picnic and once at a village dance. Our courting was then carried on by correspondence. It had reached a fine crescendo by the time he returned a few weeks later from his parents' Shropshire home to claim my hand. As he stepped off the train tension clamped the back of my neck.

"Oh, gosh, what have I done?" My romantic pipe-dream collapsed in a heap as I approached this stranger in the tweed shooting outfit.

Unable to accept the treachery of my feelings I pretended everything was still lovely and in no time we'd been all the way to Edinburgh to buy an engagement ring. The sick feeling at the back of my neck persisted, however, and at four o'clock in the morning when he, my sister, younger brother and I were supposedly all having a splendid time at the Oban Ball, I could stand the strain no longer. Leaving the dancers – men resplendent in kilts, mess dress or tails, women rather less so in long dresses with tartan sashes over their shoulders – pounding the ballroom floor to the music of the pipes, I slunk outside with my fiancé to tell him I didn't love him.

Instantly free of tension, I could see that my fiancé was not so fortunate. Convinced I was the girl he must take back to Africa he now had to adjust to the fact he'd be returning to Tanganyika on his own. It was a sad and silent young man who escorted me back to the ballroom from the Assembly Rooms garden in whose treetops the heartless dawn chorus was in full swing. After the customary breakfast of kippers and champagne we all set off on the long drive back to Kilchrenan.

Creeping into my parents' bedroom at 6 a.m. I broke the sad news.

"Mother! I don't love him any more!"

Roused in his turn from a sound sleep my father then had to get dressed and drive the young man to the railway station, a journey that because of the twists and turns of the glen road took the best part of an hour. My father's stock of small-talk, limited at the best of times, was quickly used up.

For weeks remorse at having been beastly to someone so undeserving hung over me like a shroud. It was with relief that I set off with my trunk to expiate my sins in Edinburgh.

The Royal Infirmary, one of several British hospitals built to Florence Nightingale's design, loomed up in the damp dusk of a December afternoon: clearly a fitting place for a penitent.

Instead of entering by the main doors at the top of a wide flight of steps I was dropped off by the taxi driver at a side entrance where we'd been told Sister Tutor and her Staff Nurse assistant would be waiting to greet the new intake. Then after seeing our rooms and being given time to unpack we were taken to a small dining-room where Sister delivered a homily.

"You are to be congratulated, nurses, on having been accepted for training at the Royal Infirmary. However, you must bear in mind that it is a privilege to train at the RIE and I trust your conduct will reflect this throughout your time here.

Suitably humbled, we were escorted by Sister Tutor to a nearby department store that supplied our uniforms: tough, dark-blue, short-sleeved cotton dresses, white bibbed aprons fastening at the back, white caps held on by kirbigrips, black lisle stockings and laced shoes. Nylons were still hard to find but as most of the girls had come straight from school and I from the Wrens no one minded the unglamorous stockings. Included with the uniform were capes of scarlet wool reaching down to the elbows. (These garments, we were to find out had to be removed the instant one entered a ward; they were also to be whisked off whenever the wearer was stopped in the corridor and spoken to by a Superintendent Nurse. Removing the cape was considered to be a mark of respect, like doffing one's cap.

We spent our first three months as Probationer Nurses in the Preliminary Training School, a teaching block situated some way from the wards but close to the building in which we slept. Each of us had a small bedroom containing iron bedstead, chest of drawers, cupboard, table and upright chair. Although lacking homely touches unless you could count the plain white curtains and bedspreads, our rooms were warm; and the central heating was a luxury few of us had experienced at home.

Nurses were no longer expected to clean the wards – ward maids were employed to do this – but Sister and Staff Nurse made sure we knew how to sweep the linoleum floors of our rooms properly – "Away from the feet, nurses, not towards them" – and how to dust first with a damp duster and then with a dry one. These bedrooms had to be kept immaculate. (When for the first time during this period I went back to Kilchrenan for the week-end, I felt unease as I crossed the threshold into the normal untidiness of a family home).

The clanging of a handbell wielded by Staff Nurse woke us every moring at half-past-six. Thirty minutes later we were on our knees on the bare boards of the dining-room reciting the Lord's Prayer. Then with a cup of tea and slice of bread and butter to keep us going until breakfast at nine, we found our way to the classrooms.

There was much to be absorbed: anatomy, physiology, hygiene, bandaging, how to pour medicine correctly – "Always read the label", "Never separate cork from bottle", "Always pour away from the label" etc – bed-making and general nursing that included amongst other things instruction on how to produce beef tea and how to fill an air bed.

A thick rubber monster, the latter object looked like a (cold) hot water bottle for giants and weighed a ton when filled. Once given its quota of water the air bed was heaved onto a table. The nurse had then to press her arm down the length of the rubber surface to expel the air from inside. The resulting friction caused the hairs on one's arm to cling painfully to the rubber.

Beef tea was tedious to make, involving as it did the scraping of beefsteak into tiny fragments so that these shreds could be infused in boiling water. It was, however, a great favourite with the patients, second only in popularity to the still strictly rationed tea.

It wasn't all classroom, however. During the first three months we gained experience of the real thing by spending half every Sunday on a ward, the same ward each time, each one of us being allocated to a different one. My ward was a Men's Medical, run by an efficient, respected and unsmiling Sister with whom I felt ill at ease from the word go. She wore her hair in a tight bun, its reddish colour and shape reminding me of a neat pile of horse droppings. It helped to reflect on this when she was at her most chilling. Regrettably, it wasn't to be long before this coldness turned to frost-bite in her dealings with the new probationer.

During my early days at the Infirmary and before disaster struck I went about my duties and studies in the happy knowledge I'd embarked on the finest career in the world. Walking down the Mound to window-shop in Princes Street I floated along in a state of euphoria. And a secondary sensation in those early days was that of disorientation upon emerging from the vast temple of sickness into the bustle of healthy people, or people at least not visibly suffering from either chronic bronchitis, heart disease or gastric ulcers, all much in evidence in Ward 22.

Apart from my friendship with Pam from Lancashire who was part of this new intake of nurses I failed to become close to my fellow probationers. Most had been educated at Scottish academies, well known of course for their high standards, whereas I, although of Scottish parentage, had been a pupil in what even my father described as a "snob" school. (He'd been able to manage the boarding fees because the school took two sisters for the price of one.) The difference in schooling meant I didn't speak the Scottish girls' language nor they mine. Soon, however, Pam and I became close friends and during the first year she and I spent all our free time together. She proved to be an excellent nurse, full of common sense, and although we never worked together I could tell from her anecdotes that she must have been a valuable person to have around, especially when crises arose. She later won many prizes in our class exams; unlike other prize-winners she never asked for the expected books on nursing or medicine as her reward but for anthologies of poetry or books of Gainsborough and Velasquez reproductions from the Phaedon Press.

CHAPTER 2

With the preliminary training completed we began the working day at 7.30 am and finished at 8.30 pm, with two or three hours off at some stage. The most popular "shift" covered the hours of 7.30 in the morning until 6 pm, thus allowing the nurse a free evening. Off-duty time between 9 am and 12 noon was not relished since it was during those hours that compulsory lectures were held. We were, however, given a day off every week as well as half Sunday.

Before going off duty prior to one's free day there was a little ritual to be performed. You must go into Sister's office and stand respectfully until she can spare the time to look up from her report-writing and acknowledge your presence.

"Day off tomorrow, Sister."

"Very well, Nurse," spoken with a tightening of the lips.

It was at moments such as these that I cheered myself with unspoken comments on her coiffure.

Our annual leave allowance of twenty-eight days had to be taken in two bites, the first as soon as six months' training had been completed. Therefore for the duration of our four years as student nurses our intake would have to take its holidays in May and November.

The salary of £8 a month didn't go far in spite of free board and lodging. Once I ran myself short between paydays by spending £4 on a pair of red walking shoes whose steel buckles had rendered them irresistible. Occasionally a patient would give us a tip, sometimes as much as 5/–. Some nurses considered it more seemly to put the tip into a Red Cross tin kept just inside the main doors of the ward but I kept mine. It was what the patient intended and in any case the extra cash helped.

Florence Nightingale's enthusiasm for cross-ventilation had dictated the presence of tall windows at frequent intervals down each side of the long wards. Even during the coldest weather fresh air was allowed in. The patients kept warm by wrapping themselves in body blankets while their feet rested against hot-water tins resembling long loaves made out of battered copper. These were collected twice a day by the probationer on duty. Piling them onto a large wooden trolley she'd trundle them along to the kitchen for a refill from the hot tap.

Nurses on duty weren't permitted to wear cardigans but in the winter could wear short-sleeved jerseys under their dresses. No doubt the bracing temperature inside these wards made survival difficult for heat-loving germs even if it gave us gooseflesh.

Life in the late 1940s was still austere but at the Royal Infirmary we at least ate well. We were told by Sister Tutor and came to believe it that the breakfast porridge, better than any we'd eaten at home, was remembered with nostalgia by former RIE nurses and doctors all over the world.

Jugs of milk stood on every table at lunch-time and lump-free custard flowed freely with every steamed pudding. To fill in the gaps between meals when Sister wasn't around, we'd finish off food surplus to the patients' requirements, hiding behind the kitchen door to dispose of fruit pie and custard. When I went home for a weekend our Minister's wife told me,

"You're getting quite stout, Miss Stewart."

But if we ate like horses it was because we worked like them. The length of the wards guaranteed also the covering of many miles by our sensibly-clad feet. For example, when a patient at the bottom end of the ward needed a bedpan in between bedpan rounds a pair of screens had to be fetched from a stack at the top end. Although most screens were made of calico stretched over light wooden frames some were of solid wood covered in shiny water-proof material known as American cloth. To carry these heavy objects required muscle-power.

Down at the far end of the ward and on either side of the fireplace were doors leading to two "turrets". The turret on the left contained no bows and arrows or boiling oil but a bath for patients permitted to have one. The turret on the right housed lavatories, large sinks and bedpans. Nurses weren't allowed to sit down while on duty but sometimes it was possible to go along to the turret and prop oneself on the edge of a bath for a minute or two.

In my first ward as the most junior probationer I had to collect and clean sputum mugs standing on bedside lockers. Some of the old men suffered from fearful chest complaints and since the only tools for cleaning the mugs were a bottle-brush and water from the tap, it was a horrid task.

While working one afternoon in this men's medical ward during the early days of my training I succeeded through shyness and lack of commonsense in setting in motion an event to destroy for good any self-confidence I'd acquired as an embryo nurse.

The ward was busy and as it was Sunday there were fewer nurses on duty than usual. Many of the patients were seriously ill; Mr T, in a bed near the top end, was suffering from heart failure. His lips were blue and most of the time he could only breathe with the help of an oxygen mask. Never having seen anyone in such distress before I escaped for a minute to shed some tears in the turret and pray that this man would soon be released from his ordeal. By supper time my prayer had been answered.

Patients were normally given bedpans when the need arose, but Sister felt that a commode beside Mr T's bed would make things easier for him – not that the Chief (Consultant) entirely approved. When I came on duty after lunch I was told by the Staff Nurse that Mr T wasn't to be given the commode if he asked for it: She added:
"He's just had one."
When therefore the poor man beckoned me over several hours later to say he needed to go I considered enough time had elapsed to make his request reasonable. Placing screens round his bed I helped him onto the commode. He then asked me to leave him. Respecting his need for privacy I stood outside intending to wait until he'd finished and then help him back into bed. Unfortunately, I was seen standing there apparently idle and was despatched to perform some task by one of the senior nurses.

Having accomplished whatever it was, I remembered Mr T. Hurrying back to his bed I peered round the screens to find him sitting where I'd left him. Even to my inexperienced eyes it was obvious that death had claimed him.

As I hurried off to fetch Staff Nurse it didn't occur to me that I'd blundered horribly. Staff Nurse made no reproaches and together we lifted the body onto the bed.

In due course Sister was informed, Mr T made tidy and his widow supported up to his bedside.

In her office that evening Sister grimly spelt out the extent of my failure. It might even be necessary, she said, to inform the Procurator Fiscal of this sudden death. She asked me no questions, however, and I said nothing. Her cold demeanour persuaded me that the words "I'm sorry" would be inadequate and inappropriate. This silence she took to mean indifference I later learned.

Although unable to feel remorse for having helped a doomed and suffering man into the next life a little sooner than he would otherwise have gone, I was appalled by my stupidity at leaving him on his own and then forgetting about him.

From then on I found commonsense had done a bunk, especially when Sister was on duty. Convinced she was watching my every move I felt more clueless than ever. It would no doubt have helped if I'd been able to talk to someone in the Infirmary about what had happened but such an opportunity was not forthcoming.

The Procurator Fiscal wasn't mentioned again and if the Chief gave

Sister a bad time over the commode business she said nothing to me. A veil was drawn over the regrettable episode.

It was with tremendous relief that I heard one morning I must report to a new ward.

In this Women's Medical bedpans featured largely in the daily life of the probationer nurses. And it was during my spell in this ward that I received a boost to a negligible self-esteem by being given the title of Bedpan Queen.

After every meal a screen is placed in front of the main double doors of the ward indicating to those outside that an eagerly-awaited bedpan round is in progress. The probationer nurse, wearing a white overall fastened at the back, sprints out of the turret with a stack of warmed bedpans to be slipped under the raised bottoms. The simplest system is to work methodically down the two rows of beds but sometimes a patient in desperate need is allowed to jump the queue.

The last bedpan having been given out, some of the first will have been finished with. Back to the turret goes the bedpan covered with a towel. Having flushed away the contents and given a quick brush round to the inside of the bedpan the most popular nurse of the moment speeds off to the next customer.

Each patient's output of urine was kept in a chamber pot secreted in the small cupboard beside her bed. These collections were emptied during the night by the junior nurse on duty. A tricky business, as I was to discover upon my return to the ward on night duty, because in order to save journeys it was necessary to carry several jerries at a time, one on top of the other. Once on its way turret-wards the urine would start to slipslop about, mounting higher and higher up the sides of the heavy china chamber until risk of spillage forced one to slow down.

Giving a patient a beep as we called bedpans could cause nail-biting for a nurse if a patient needed one when the Chief's rounds were imminent – would she be able to finish before the screens had to be removed and the ward doors flung open to admit the Chief with his entourage of doctors and medical students? Knowing that they must be lying tidily in their beds under the smoothed-out white bedspreads when this august person made his entrance, the patients did their best to cooperate.

The Chiefs were the only people not in awe of the ward sisters, several of whom had earned themselves the prefix of "bitchy". If a student nurse told a friend she was being shifted to such-and-such a ward, the other might say:

"Bad luck, that's Bitchy So-and-So's ward."

Some sisters, of course, were not like this and I could willingly have spent my entire training in one of the gynae wards. Perhaps the pressures there were less than in some of the others but the Sister in charge was kind and courteous towards us. For three months I felt capable and dependable.

CHAPTER 3

Shortly before the close of 1948 the governors of the Royal Infirmary gave the nurses their annual Christmas dinner. Wearing a black pin-striped suit with wing collar and reminding me in retrospect of the Fat Controller in Thomas the Tank Engine, one of the governors addressed us after the meal. He thanked us all for our hard work and regretted that this would be the last such dinner since the RIE was soon to become part of the new National Health Service.

Whatever the status to be enjoyed shortly by the Infirmary, Christmas day began as always with hundreds of nurses getting up at 5 am to sing carols. The procession of young women in their scarlet capes moved slowly along the wide corridors past open ward doors, singing as they went. So great were our numbers that nurses singing "O come, all ye faithful" at the front were half a verse ahead of those at the back, with resulting confusion in the middle ranks.

Another Christmas tradition dictated that each ward Resident (doctor) be given a stocking filled with joky presents, the ruder the better. Our young man was shy, as was the Staff Nurse who made the presentation; and so unfortunately were the rest of us. More embarrassment than merriment prevailed as he opened his stocking but the strained atmosphere was relieved when in burst a wheel-chair, propelled by a medical student. In the chair huddled a student disguised as a heavily-pregnant woman. His groans and falsetto complaints of "awfee" back-pains delighted the women patients.

In January 1949 our intake began its first spell of night duty. No longer probationers we had become Junior Blue-Frocks, JBs for short.

This advance in rank was indicated by a blue strip sewn onto the sleeve and the stiff white belt we were now permitted to wear. From this time on also I all but lost the companionship of Pam.

During her first year she'd missed many weeks of training through illness. As a result she wasn't ready to begin night duty with the rest of us. Often, therefore, when she was on duty I'd be sleeping, and vice versa.

Together in our first year we'd gone skating and swimming and had consumed substantial teas in Mackies, Princes Street. We'd also taken in a modest amount of culture in this the second year of the International Festival. French films were then much in vogue, as were Italian films of opera. Especially enjoyable was the one of Pagliacci, particularly when the lovers are both in the river, singing gloriously and carrying on in an erotic fashion. We also found Robert Helpmann and Margot Fonteyn pretty impressive as they danced to music by Cesar Franck.

But it was on my own that I saw a film which reinforced my belief that I mustn't give up this self-imposed ordeal of a job. The film was entitled "Monsieur Vincent". Vincent de Paul, a French aristocrat living in the 17th century, had become a priest. Early in the film he's invited for an afternoon's outing in a rich friend's galley. The friend has the merry idea of challenging another galley owner to a race. So, urged on by the thudding of a drum the oarsmen are forced to row ever faster with their tree-like oars. When one of these slaves collapses Monsieur Vincent can bear it no longer: he rushes down from his canopied seat in the stern, grabs the abandoned oar and to his friend's shocked astonishment rows in the dead man's place. Not long after this episode he leaves his life of comparative comfort to spend the rest of his days sharing the existence of the destitute.

Emerging from the cinema on the heels of a troop of nuns who have evidently been given a special dispensation to go to the pictures. I decided being unhappy in my nurse's life and lonely from seeing Pam so rarely were insufficent reasons for quitting. This lofty sentiment was one of two factors to keep me at the RIE for another year.

CHAPTER 4

My three-month spell of night duty took place first on the orthopaedic ward and then on the already familiar women's medical ward. The nights there whizzed past since there was much to get done and by 4 o'clock we'd start washing patients unable to sleep or so ill they couldn't tell what time of day it was. Thirty-five beds had to be made, bedpans given out, bowls of hot water taken to those able to wash themselves and everything must be tidied away before the day staff appeared at half past seven. Since there were only two of us on duty, accomplishing these tasks involved a fight against the clock, especially if a patient had died during the night. Extra help for the laying-out procedure was usually given when this happened.

Mattresses were hard, made increasingly so by the heavy rubber sheeting placed under the tough, coarse sheet. Bed-sores were kept at bay through the administration of back-rubs after each bedpan round. The patient's lower back would be briskly rubbed, first with soapy water and then, when dried with the patient's towel, with meths to toughen the skin. The biceps I developed in my right arm from carrying out this activity would have done credit to a body-builder.

When the three months were up we moved from the quiet house reserved for night duty staff to a different accommodation block. Our previous Nurses' Home had consisted of a glass-fronted, one-storey building resembling a conservatory and spurned by domestic staff because of the damp. Situated over a bakery the latest one was at least warm and dry but proved to have a disadvantage: my room attracted visits from a bold and unusually large mouse who ate holes in my Stewart tartan woollen dress. I suspected he was also responsible for the two fleas I found on my bed. When I mentioned the latter to the Sister in charge of the Home she dismissed my complaint with the words,

"You must have brought them in yourself, Nurse!"

Returning to day duty I was told to report to a men's surgical ward. My heart sank since the Sister in charge wasn't known for her amiability. She was however famous throughout the Infirmary for the non-touch technique she employed while changing the dressings of post-operative patients. Her skill enabled her to do these in record time, moving as she did from one patient to another without having to scrub up in between since the sterile forceps held in her gloved hands did all the work. Having completed a dressing she would be handed a clean pair of forceps with which to start on the next patient.

I'd been working in this ward for a few days only when by some mischance the only nurse available to assist the expert was Stewart. It went badly. Apart from having been shown how to in training school, I'd had no experience of taking gloves, forceps and swabs out of a casket (sterilisation drum) by means of a pair of jumbo-sized forceps. More than once I succeeded in dropping whatever it was Sister was impatiently waiting to he handed or, worse still, I touched the sterile cloth she'd placed beside the patient's wound. A new cloth had then to be produced. With Sister's displeasure mounting to an alarming degree, I had the feeling that at any minute I was going to erupt into hysterical laughter. I knew well how inept I was being but a little forbearance on her part might have calmed my jangled nerves as well as her own.

Somehow we stumbled through to the end: Sister stamped off to breakfast and the ward relaxed.

Penicillin in those days was given the hard way, i.e. into the buttock. Having such injections every three or four hours for several days was not a nice experience, especially for those who didn't possess a well-padded behind. A young miner injured in a pit accident refused at first to have anything to do with the formidably large syringe when it was brought to his bedside. I assured him he wouldn't feel the needle go in, just a thump from the heel of my hand followed by a sensation of bruising. To my relief he accepted this reassurance and submitted to the injection. I myself had been grateful for the thumping strategy while in the nurses' sick room having a course of injections for boils. I also knew what it was like to be injected by a nurse who placed the point of the needle against the skin and then pushed it in as though it were a long drawing pin. That hurt.

Lumbar punctures for drawing off cerebrospinal fluid featured frequently in the medical wards. Sometimes this procedure didn't cause the patient much discomfort and sometimes it did. After administering a local anaesthetic the doctor would insert the large-bore needle into the patient's spine and it was soon after this that a patient might begin to wince and groan. I'd then become giddy in sympathy, only just managing to last out until the aspiration of fluid had been completed and assistance at the bedside was no longer required. Groping my way to the turret it would be head-between-the-knees time for a minute or two before a return to the ward looking an interesting shade of grey-mauve – I knew because I hadn't been able to resist a quick glance in the turret mirror.

A piece of nursemanship instilled into us was used when, as sometimes happened, a patient suffering from a gastric ulcer vomited dried blood. The first thing we had to do was cover the mess on the bedclothes with a towel, thereby sparing the patient an alarming sight.

We were also trained to treat with reverence the bodies of those who'd died, to speak as little as possible, and then in quiet tones. This behaviour hadn't been acquired by everyone, however. One day two porters came to fetch a young woman who'd died that morning and was to be prepared for burial by her own people. The porters flung her body onto the trolley, one of them remarking:

"Jewish, ain't she?"

In those days to become a State Registered Nurse took four years and it was at the half-way mark that I went home for a two-week holiday. As I sat on the window seat watching the rain hammering onto the surface of Loch Awe it came to me that there was no law insisting I slog on with an experience I was finding increasingly bleak. Although I got on well with most of the patients and found satisfaction in the work of caring for them I never lost the conviction that sooner or later some crisis would arise for which I would prove totally inadequate; nor could I stick for much longer the isolation in which I found myself. My friend was no longer available to gossip with in off-duty hours and in spite of rubbing shoulders every day with young doctors and medical students from the University I had no boy-friend. My unrelaxed manner and anxious expression must have been a turn-off.

The prospect of returning to this life was unbearable. I decided not to go back! It was no way to pull out – I ought to give a month's notice – but the decision made me rejoice, as though granted a reprieve from a prison sentence. Having got away, I was not going to return, even for a day.

My father, loving but reserved and difficult to talk to, hadn't known I was anything but happy as a student nurse because I'd never mentioned my feelings to him or to anyone else for that matter. We had after all been brought up not to make a fuss. It was a surprise and a relief, therefore, when he took my defection calmly. The wish not to disappoint Daddy had been even more potent in keeping me at it than had the inspiration of "Monsieur Vincent".

PART III

LAGOS, NIGERIA
March 1955–July 1956

CHAPTER 1

At home following a stay in Canada I sat amongst the breakfast things reading the situations vacant column in the Telegraph to see what was on offer for secretaries.

I'd taken a week's refresher course at St James's Secretarial College (the snobbish-sounding "For Gentlewomen" had by then been dropped from its title) and a friend with a flat in Putney had suggested I try for a job as secretary to an MP. Lacking interest in politics, however, I could not work up enthusiasm for such a career, whereas "Secretary required for old-established commercial firm in Lagos, Nigeria..." sounded worth pursuing. According to the advertisement the secretary would be provided with a flat and a car. Irresistible.

Possession of the usual secretarial qualifications wasn't all that was demanded: to be considered for the job one had to be at least 28 years old and have experienced life in a hot climate. Since I qualified in all respects I sent off a letter of application. In due course a letter came back inviting me for interview at the Head Office in Liverpool.

I booked a room in a temperance hotel on the advice of an elderly friend, who also told me what size tip to leave on the mantelpiece for the chambermaid – a shilling she considered appropriate. As dusk was falling in the late January afternoon I was met at Liverpool station by Miss Edwards, Personnel Officer from John Holt.

A woman in her early forties dressed in sensible tweeds she shook me by the hand with much warmth and suggested after I'd eaten she come back for me and we go to the cinema. This we did and the film, starring Joyce Grenfell as a St Trinian's games mistress, made me cry from laughing so much I could hardly see the screen....

Next day I found my way to the John Holt building on the waterfront to be interviewed by the General Manager. During our conversation he described the sort of life led by expatriates in Lagos, mentioning in passing the Ikoyi Club – evidently the hub of Lagos social life – and I asked whether Nigerians could become members.

"No, unfortunately, except for one or two exceptions".

I was then introduced to the Sales Manager in need of a secretary. Nice-looking with blue eyes and moustache he spoke with a lah-di-dah accent.

"It's demned hot in Lagos" he warned.

In spite of this I took to him and was pleased to be offered the job soon after my return to Fife.

Down from the attic came the trunk once more, this time to be packed with clothes suitable for Africa, a country familiar to me only through school geography books and the National Geographic.

The first tour of duty was to be of eighteen months' duration followed by three months' home leave. It was of course hoped and expected that one would return to Lagos for a second tour.

The only other woman in the Lagos office apart from a personnel officer was the Managing Director's secretary. She wrote to me from Nigeria with suggestions as to what clothes I should bring. The social life for single girls being all that one could wish she advised me to pack at least two long evening dresses. Dances in the Club could be formal affairs. Having little money I could afford to buy one dress only and of course the pink taffeta and lace would have been all wrong in the humid heat. The good quality Horrockses cotton dress I bought was to prove equally wrong since its densely-woven material trapped the air, producing a Turkish-bath effect for my legs.

My future colleague failed to warn me that as soon as I arrived in Lagos I'd need plenty of money for basic household items such as a dustbin that the Company did not see fit to supply. She probably assumed I'd have enough nous to come out with more than £5 in my purse.

The MV Apapa, one of three combined passenger and cargo ships belonging to the Elder Dempster Line, made regular voyages from Liverpool to Lagos and back, calling in at British West African ports on the way. I found I was to share a two-berth cabin with a girl setting off to Africa as a trainee missionary. This fact made it easy for me to say my prayers without embarrassment before getting into bed at night, but the length of time she spent on her knees was awe-inspiring.

Beside my companion's bunk were two bouquets of flowers and on my bunk lay one for me with a card indicating it was from the nice Miss Edwards. I resolved she would not regret having taken me on.

For the first five days of a voyage that had started on the 24th March 1955 the sea was rough, each day to be endured rather than enjoyed. Following a routine call at Las Palmas, however, the ship entered calm waters, the grey of the sky changed to blue. With a sore throat newly acquired preventing me from speaking in more than a whisper, I lay beside the swimming-pool basking in the sun while idly watching passengers of all ages jumping in and out of the water.

A young man in blue bathing-trunks heaved himself out of the pool to flop down beside me. Introducing himself he told me he was returning to Lagos to continue his career as manufacturers' representative. Prior to this he'd spent two tours of duty behind the counter in the Bank of British West Africa, first in northern Nigeria and then in Lagos.

We agreed to meet for a drink that evening before going along to the Carnival Dance to be held on the boat deck. At lunch that day I glanced across the dining-room and saw that John shared a table with several other young men. As our friendship progressed John told me that one of the first things he'd done on coming aboard was to examine the passenger list. Seeing the name "Miss Stewart" he'd determined to be the one to take charge of this unattached female. Lagos was a lonely place for a young man on his own.

We talked on the dance floor and we talked in the moonlight by the ship's rail. We felt comfortable with each other and by the time the ship docked we were engaged. A certain element of physical excitement was missing but I remembered my mother's words –

"That side of marriage is not important, dear!"

– and shoved to the back of my mind any tiny doubts. All the same I was a little uneasy about the speed with which the courtship was being conducted but no one had ever before pursued me with such single-mindedness, (I didn't count the courtship by correspondence eight years previously.) If John felt we were right for each other then it must be so. Stewart-marker was about to fall in again, not of course onto a spot marked in chalk but into the married state.

We disembarked at the port of Apapa, Lagos where I was met by John Holt Nigeria's personnel officer. She accompanied me into the hangar-like building on the dockside. In a crowd of European men, mostly British, wearing the colonial uniform of long shorts, shirts and white knee-socks, and Nigerians (some dressed the same and others in ankle-length robes with pushed-back sleeves) we found our luggage piled onto trestle tables.

Noise boomed around us as Nigerians greeted returning friends and relations. One of these was a young woman who'd spent several years in England becoming a State Registered Nurse. A quiet person during the voyage she had come into her own back in her own country and I saw her strutting off in a tight white suit, picture hat and high heels, surrounded by admirers.

When John, a personable young man obviously knowing the ropes, introduced himself to the personnel officer, she gave me the keys to my flat and with directions as to its location left me in John's care. His African assistant was waiting outside with a Standard van into whose interior our luggage was loaded.

The London-based firm John worked for as a Manufacturers' Representative, or bag-man as he and his colleagues preferred to call themselves, were agents for a supplier of veterinary products as well as such firms as Yardley and Smedley. John's sales territory encompassed the whole of Nigeria and although perhaps lacking prestige the job suited him.

My flat was on the ground floor of a two-storeyed building and within this suburb of Ikoyi lived other expatriates in varying degrees of grandeur, the drabness of the area relieved by trees and flowering shrubs. Golf course and Club lay conveniently to hand.

Waiting to meet me was Dixon, cook/house-boy provided by the Company. To help him with the rough he had an assistant, a well-built young man named Dick, bearing the inappropriate title of Small Boy. Promising to return later John left to check into his one-star hotel.

Half-way through my unpacking Dixon, who spoke pidgin-English (for some reason in those days the colonial British in West Africa considered that African servants should be taught this quaint form of speech rather than correct English) presented me with a list of kitchen utensils and cleaning equipment. Almost immediately I was going to have to ask for a salary advance so that by the time I'd earned my first monthly pay of £57 there was little of it left.

Government employees in Lagos enjoyed a sensible working routine of 7 am start and 2 pm finish. For those employed by commercial firms the day started at 8 and ended at 5.30, with a two-hour break for lunch and siesta. The newly-constructed building smelling of fresh concrete into which John Holt Nigeria had recently moved its offices was hot and unattractive inside and out. Above our desks ceiling fans stirred the heat, at the same time sending any paper not anchored down flying about in an irritating fashion.

When shortly before the first World War my uncle arrived in Lagos to help set up the general hospital people had known how to construct buildings that kept out the heat. Many of these buildings with their sloping roofs and deep verandahs were still being used by government personnel. To be "Government" rather than "Commercial" had practical advantages as well as social cachet.

CHAPTER 2

Lagos was built on the shores of a lagoon, not blue as the word might suggest but the colour of mud. Along the verges gangs of prisoners from the local gaol were sometimes seen at work. Dressed in khaki shorts and shirts they cut the coarse grass with synchronised movements of long strips of metal chanting as they did so. The ability to cut grass with these home-made tools without digging up chunks of turf must have taken skill.

During his time in Nigeria John had come to love the game of polo. In the belief that I could do no better than to become a part of the scene he took me to the Polo Club the first Saturday after my arrival in Lagos. Before you could say "overdraft" I'd become not just a member but the temporary owner of a mount, a disagreeable Arab stallion named Golightly. Being in charge of this animal while its mistress was in England for six months was to prove an unexpected drain on my purse. Not only were there the groom's wages to pay but also maddeningly frequent vet's bills. Although these were for small amounts I lacked the experience to judge whether or not the veterinary product had really been needed.

Like his groom Golightly recognised an unhorsey person when he met one and the rapport supposed to exist between horse and rider failed to develop. In fact we regarded each other with mutual dislike. But I was stuck with him.

The streets of Lagos were crowded with Yorubas from central Nigeria, Ebos from the east and Hausas from the north, all drawn to this hot-bed of wheeler-dealing where much money could be made. The din of horns from car and mammy-wagon, as the buses were called, competed with the shrill ringing of hundreds of bicycle bells. Smells from open drains made one gag.

Dark and cluttered shops owned by Lebanese and Syrians overflowed onto the street. Their male assistants, John told me, were driven into work each day from the hostels in which they lived and they weren't allowed out on the town. To toil in their bosses' emporia was as much of a life as they could expect as long as they remained in Lagos.

Fulfilling the needs of expatriates, especially after pay-day, a modern department store called Kingsway and owned by the United Africa Company stocked imported clothes and household goods. Also on offer were luxuries such as silver-plated coffee spoons three sets of which we were to receive as wedding presents.

Each time an Elder Dempster ship arrived from Liverpool, Kingsway's grocery department blossomed for a while with displays of Walls sausages and Aberdeen kippers.

My engagement ring, a ruby flanked by two small diamonds, came from Kingsway although I'd tried to convince John I didn't want one. I'd been put right off them during a four-month spell as secretary in London, Ontario.

The girl who gets her man and becomes engaged over the week-end prances into the office on a Monday morning triumphantly flashing her trophy. So-and-so has "got her diamond!" is the cry amongst the typewriters, followed by a rush to gaze at this proof of desirability, the size or lack of it not being overlooked. I'd therefore decided if I became engaged again I wouldn't have a ring. John couldn't afford to buy one anyway. However, he insisted, confessing later that it was partly because he wanted to make it clear that this particular young woman was booked.

Formally engaged, therefore, we discussed the timing of our wedding. I assumed it would take place in Fife when I'd finished my eighteen-month tour. John, however, felt there was no point in waiting that long. The logical move was for us both to depart from Lagos in December when he'd be taking home leave and we'd get married then.

Always respectful of authority I felt uneasy at the prospect of breaking a contract before it was half completed. But if this was what John wanted me to do, I'd put his wishes first.

The conviction that a wife owed her husband one hundred per cent allegiance gave me the nerve to inform the Managing Director I'd be pulling out in December. He was speechless for a moment or two but when he'd recovered his comments were restrained. He no doubt recognised a lost cause when he met it.

The necessity to let my employers know John's and my plans at such an early stage arose from a need to have everything out in the open. I couldn't have stood the strain of nursing a guilty secret. Unsurprisingly, no company car came my way; for much of the remaining time with John Holt I had to depend on neighbours for lifts.

In the flat Dixon and the Small Boy had an easy time looking after their employer. To the annoyance of some of my neighbours I spoilt my two servants by allowing them to be off duty by 8 o'clock most evenings. I didn't subscribe to the custom of keeping them waiting in the kitchen until 10 or so just in case I needed a bed-time drink.

Although Dixon and I got on well enough it was for John he performed a curtsey-like obeisance when the Master returned from one of his selling tours. An endearing habit of Dixon's not necessarily unique to him was the way in which if I hurt myself in some trivial way, perhaps by banging my head on the corner of a cupboard, he'd at once say "Sorry, Madam!" Appealing also was his way of holding out both hands, one on top of the other, when accepting a gift, much as we do when receiving the bread at Holy Communion.

Two of the Nigerians at work – grey-haired office boys – used this gesture when I gave them a present to celebrate with me the fact that I'd received a telegram from John suggesting a date for our wedding. This was to be even earlier than in December. Why wait, I asked John, when I've got a flat and you are having to stay in not-very-salubrious hotels? I therefore asked for and was given permission by my employer for John to move in with me once we were married.

The 9th July was fixed with the church. More at ease with Daniel and Samson than with anyone else in Lagos, I shared my excitement with them by giving Daniel, who enjoyed a drink, a bottle of Gordon's gin and Samson a £5 note.

CHAPTER 3

John and I were married in the Colonial Church the day after John returned from a tour of Northern Nigeria. During his absence I'd spent my free time organising the wedding. This included having fittings at the dressmaker for a short, white broderie anglaise dress, sending out invitations, ordering a bouquet of frangipani and arranging for a supply of Mum's champagne (on sale or return) to be sent to the flat. At John's request I'd bought a plain gold band since there'd be no time for him to do that himself. I'd considered ordering an imported cake from Kingsway but as neither of us had any money to speak of and the cake would have been expensive our guests would have to make do with one locally made. (It was to taste more like suet pudding than cake).

My conventional upbringing persuaded me that in the absence of parent or relative it was appropriate to ask my boss to give me away. It's unlikely that the request afforded him any pleasure, knowing as he did that I'd be pushing off in December, but he agreed to do so.

John's first act when he returned from his travels was to dash into town to buy a suit at Kingsway. Locally – tailored trousers with shirt and tie would not have done. There was little choice in the shop and no time for alterations; the pale grey suit he came away with had been designed for someone less lean than John.

That evening we were invited to the home of my boss and his wife. A drink or two on an empty stomach soon removed any feelings of constraint on my part; having lost all sense of judgment I asked our host if John and I might be driven away in his spacious company car. Any one of our friends would of course be glad to give him and his wife a lift to the flat.

In the belief that this man and his extremely pleasant spouse were entering into the spirit of the thing I pointed out to them how delightful it would be for John and me to leave the church in style rather than in a van. Agreement apparently having been reached over this detail, we all parted on cordial terms.

The following morning as my next-door neighbour adjusted the veil she'd lent me and I stood admiring my reflection in the mirror, there was a knock at the door. The driver employed by our host of the previous evening stood there with a note in his hand. Puzzled, I opened the envelope. The message was chilling: my boss had been so shocked by my impertinent request to borrow his car he'd been rendered speechless. He naturally could not entertain the idea of our being driven away from the church in his vehicle while he and his wife followed in someone else's. We were however welcome to share the car with them after the service and no more would be said.

Humiliation crept over me as I read these words but by the time the gentleman in question arrived at my door, all smiles, and ready to escort me to the church I had recovered from the shock. Nevertheless, it had been a nasty start to the day.

As we swept up to the porch, rain was beginning to fall. But the service went as it should, with Bach's Toccata and Fugue played with gusto by an amateur organist to send us off down the aisle as man and wife. We came to a halt on the church steps, the guests having had a job to keep up with us, the bride with her bouquet of frangipani held in the wrong hand, the ink on her marriage certificate already smudged by the drizzle.

The reception took place in my flat and, since we could have counted on one hand the number of friends as opposed to acquaintances we had in Lagos, many of the guests were people I scarcely knew but they were happy to come along to a party. My giver-away and his wife departed as soon as they decently could.

While we all drank a horrible combination of champagne, rum and coca cola, I showed off by pretending to smoke with a long black holder. Two hours later John and I drove away not in the van but in a borrowed Fiat, once some wags had had their fun heaving up the rear end of the car several feet from the ground.

We couldn't afford to go to a hotel so we drove round Lagos a few times, returning when we knew all our guests would have departed. In our absence Dixon and Dick had restored the flat to its usual tidy state. After a heavy sleep we awoke feeling frail but strong enough to open and eat a tin of bamboo shoots from John's store of samples.

Two days later John and his assistant set off on another sales tour. For company during the evenings I had a young African Grey parrot. Named Zik after a Nigerian politician he at first produced nothing but squawking noises. Then one evening as I sat eating my supper I was startled by the sound of a small voice announcing "Soup's ready!", the not very elegant way in which Dick announced supper on Dixon's half-day. Although never to repeat these words Zik soon learnt to wolf-whistle and to say "Stop it!", "How d'ya do" and, with an exaggeratedly refined accent. "Hellao". Like others of his breed he liked to imitate the plop of a cork being drawn and the gloopgloops that followed. (Later in London he learnt to reproduce with dreadful accuracy the sound of my father-in-law's bronchial cough).

While drinking coffee one Saturday morning with a neighbour whose husband also worked for John Holt I was given a demonstration on how to deal with servants. The young woman had discovered some commodity or other was missing from the larder. Summoning the cook in shrill tones she proceeded to give him a tongue-lashing in the belief that this inspired awe and respect. The cook was too polite to shout back but I could tell from his expression that he viewed her behaviour with amusement rather than contrition.

This impression was reinforced by Jimmo, one of the Company's chauffeurs. One sultry afternoon when nothing much was happening he sauntered into my office for a chat. In fact I let the side down by allowing him to comment on certain members of the expatriate staff but I couldn't resist hearing what he thought. Dignified people as a rule Nigerians deplored a lack of dignity in those who should have known better. Jimmo may only have been a driver but he disliked bad manners as much as anyone. Immaculately turned out in white shirt and well-creased trousers, he left me to my typing, trailing behind him a pleasing smell of after-shave.

That some Madams, as we were addressed by our servants, throve on running battles with their boys was indisputable. The contents of the store cupboard provided a rich source of suspicion and acrimony. Sugar lumps were counted after breakfast and a note made of the level of whisky remaining in the bottle at the end of each day. Nagging the servants possibly helped pass the time.

As I unpacked on my first evening I made the disagreeable discovery that the flat was home to jumbo-sized cockroaches. Having been unaware that such monsters were part of the Lagos scene I recoiled in horror at the first sighting. Several inches long, dark brown and shiny, the creature possessed whiskers as long as its body, turning these whiskers to left and to right as it sought an escape route. This sign of intelligence merely enhanced the sinister aspect of the cockroach.

With a broom constructed like a birch I chased the intruder round the bedroom eventually forcing it into a corner where I killed it. This activity proved to be a nightly routine before I could climb into bed under the mosquito net, tucking in the edges under the mattress so that nothing could creep in. And although I soon became accustomed to the cockroaches I never failed to jump when one popped out of the washbasin overflow while I was bending over to shampoo my hair.

Drinking Star beer in the sitting-room one airless evening, the front door open wide, John and I were visited by a more repellent visitor than the cockroach.

Straight out of a horror movie, in scuttled a party of land-crabs. These inhabitants of reclaimed land adjoining the lagoon, with their long thin, spider-like legs supporting smallish grey bodies, were out for an evening's scavenge.

John sprang out of his chair, grabbed a polo stick and drove away the visitors, their claws clicking on the tiled floor as they skittered out into the darkness. We kept the front door shut from then on.

One exciting consequence of my association with Golightly, that other specimen of Nigerian fauna, was the sensation of breaking the sound barrier he periodically allowed me to experience. His absent mistress I was told did not allow him to move any faster than at a trot during his daily exercise. Both Golightly and I found this boring. He was only too pleased to be urged into a canter, but there was a snag: the canter invariably turned into an uncontrollable gallop. It was exhilarating as round and round the edge of the polo field we'd tear with the wind roaring past my ears. At these times Golightly was boss and I could only wait until he ran out of steam. Like a cheetah he didn't seem able to keep the furious pace up for long. Just as well, since his mouth was lined with leather and no amount of pulling on my part could persuade him to slow down until he chose to.

Once when the gallop had as usual degenerated into a bolt we rocketed up to his stable. Having been told that horses were known to have galloped right into their stables and realising where he was heading, I was worried; visions of decapitation flashed through my mind. Fortunately Golightly decided to come to a halt in the stable yard and a collision between door lintel and my head was averted.

On another occasion we took a path leading past the golf course. Surely this time I'd be able to control him once we ventured into a canter. But no: back went his ears and we were off. Scattering pedestrians and poultry we thundered along to finish up in front of the Club pavilion where members were enjoying a gin and tonic after their game of polo. At this very spot Golightly jammed on his brakes, causing me to fly over his head and land face down in the grubby sand.

No harm was done except to my image but I knew what it was to bite the dust. While I spat out the dirt and picked myself up Golightly seized the opportunity to eat as much of the parasite-laden grass as he could before I was able to grab the reins and stop him.

A disapproving silence from the Club members underlined this lack of horsemanship and I was grateful to a young army officer who made a joke out of it by asking,

"Who gave you permission to dismount, Mrs Wood?"

On his return from a tour of selling John was to hear all about Golightly's proclivity for bolting. Experienced rider though he was he too found it difficult to control the animal once it had made up its mind to take off.

When the owner returned from her extended leave at the end of September my six-month Golightly-minding came to an end. Thankfully I threw away my jodhpurs that by this time were looking pretty silly, the legs having shrunk to half-way up my shins.

December came and with it my goodbyes to John Holt Nigeria. The General Manager over on a visit from Liverpool surprised me by his mildness, saying he quite understood I must leave with my husband. I heard later, however, that in Liverpool Head Office the name of Stewart had become synonymous with disaster.

CHAPTER 4

Christmas was spent with my parents in Fife. Then following a late honeymoon skiing in Murren we lived for a month in the unaccustomed luxury of a furnished flat in Ebury Street.

Attending as many theatre productions as possible was what people did in those days when on leave from the colonies. Our choice included The Reluctant Debutante, Kismet (during which the heating broke down – performers and audience froze) and Waiting for Godot – right over my head. During these four weeks John went off every day to his employer's West End office while I took driving lessons in the Earl's Court Road. To my instructor's surprise, and with time running out before our return to Nigeria, I passed the test.

Then back to Lagos, this time by air. John found a villa to rent in the suburb of Apapa. One of our first visitors was Dixon. He'd heard we'd returned and was presenting himself for work. Although dour, he was honest and dependable and we were glad to take him back; a small building in the compound provided his living quarters.

When John and I had settled in Dixon asked me one morning to drive him to his village so that he could collect his load, by which he meant bedding, small pieces of furniture and kitchen utensils. He assured me that the village wasn't far away, telling me what I wanted to hear rather than the truth. One afternoon, therefore, when John didn't need the van Dixon and I set off.

Several miles from Lagos the tarmac'd surface gave out and we were bumping along reddish-coloured laterite hard and corrugated. Although this was rough, worse awaited us as we plunged into the bush along a track only just wide enough for our vehicle. Trees and thickets scraped the sides of the van. At one point Dixon got out with his machete to hack away at obstructing branches. By then my principal fear was that darkness would close in by the time we reached our destination, necessitating an overnight stay in the bush. Although sure of a welcome from Dixon's family and friends I feared the mosquitoes. However, with a couple of hours of daylight still in hand, we broke through into a clearing and there was a village of small white-washed houses with corrugated-iron roofs.

Helped by friends who'd obviously been expecting him, Dixon quickly loaded the pile of possessions stacked outside a small wooden house. Last to go in was a double mattress; between it and the van's roof a young woman then squeezed herself. Dixon hadn't mentioned that his wife was to be part of his load.

As we emerged from the bush onto the laterite track darkness fell, but in spite of not having driven at night before I no longer worried. We were heading in the right direction and when at last the van's headlights shone on the welcome sight of our Apapa villa I couldn't help feeling I'd been rather clever.

During one of his sales tours John met a director of Pearl & Dean the cinema advertising firm. Looking for someone to manage the Lagos end of the business this man offered the position to John who immediately accepted. He'd have less travelling, he'd get a higher salary, his rent would be paid and there would be a car for his use. In due course John took up his position as manager of the Pearl & Dean Lagos office.

Nigerian cinema audiences relished the advertisements, shouting their appreciation as old favourites appeared on the screen. Nigerian mothers were urged to feed their babies on a powdered milk called Klim – more sophisticated than breast milk – and to give their families white bread and margarine instead of the maize on which they'd been thriving all their lives.

Cinemas throughout the country ordered advertising reels through the Lagos office and going to the pictures to check up on the ads became a frequent pastime for us. On one expedition to an open-air cinema, just when the film was becoming exciting the audience had to flee. A passing night-soil cart had had a collision, spilling its contents all over the street.

One day when all seemed to be going well, with little warning and no explanation a second director arrived from London to work in the Lagos office. As far as John knew he'd been doing an effective job but this man relegated him to the status of clerk, telling him also that he mustn't regard the car as being for his use exclusively: he could only have it when the man didn't need it himself. Apart from the inconvenience of being without transport, for an expatriate in Lagos not to have a car of his own was to lose face indeed.

John's frustration and unhappiness at work were then compounded by shocking domestic news: his wife was pregnant. Chatting on the Apapa's boatdeck about the piccins we'd have and the kindly Nigerian mammy who'd help look after them was one thing: the reality for John was another. He was horrified; he felt too young to be undertaking fatherhood and persuaded himself I'd only married him in order to have a baby. This was hard to disprove since I was overjoyed at being pregnant. At least though we were united in our disenchantment with Lagos and decided it was time to return to the UK for good.

John succeeded in finding a new employer for Dixon and before we left I gave him one or two small objects he asked for "....to remember you by, Madam". These included an alarm clock but not for some reason the Penguin Cookery Book he coveted. This meanness on my part has bothered me ever since.

Zik stood on his swing, holding on to the side of it with his claw, regarding the dockside scene with interest as we boarded a small German cargo ship. John had fixed up our passage with the captain who was letting us have the two-berth cabin normally kept as sickbay for the crew.

We ate our meals with the captain and his officers, the captain alone speaking English: my one year of School Certificate German didn't help much. The voyage to Rotterdam took three weeks and time dragged. All we could do was to play cards in our cabin or read the paperbacks we'd brought with us.

Zik wasn't bored. He revelled in the movement of the ship as we entered rough seas but it made me tremendously sick. Rotterdam hove in sight eventually and upon disembarking I was surprised to find that the dock appeared to be moving up and down in a disagreeable fashion. Having adapted to the rolling of the ship we had to get used to the stability of the land. Our train to The Hook was rock-steady, however, and having crossed by ferry to Harwich we finally made it to South London.

PART IV

LONDON, ONTARIO AND NEW YORK CITY

1957–1961

CHAPTER 1

The taxi dropped us, Zik and the luggage at a boarding-house close to the home of John's parents in Clapham. A few streets away from their own address my father-in-law had found a place for us to rent: the middle two floors of a terraced house in Union Road. We couldn't move in straight away since the place was dingey, untouched by paintbrush since before the war, but at £4 a week the rent was modest.

When John and his father had finished scraping, wallpapering and painting, and had laid in kitchen and bathroom heavy-duty floor covering that apart from the odd dent where machinery had stood on it looked brand new, our home I considered showed excellent taste.

The sitting-room with its tall sash windows, second-hand sofa and matching armchairs upholstered in blue brocade and smelling faintly of perfume would no doubt have earned the approval of the original late-Victorian occupants. And with the addition of an antique pedestal table and mahogany bureau costing at £12 more than we could afford, the room might have been overlooking Holland Park rather than a bagwash and Express Dairy.

John didn't believe in buying new if he could get it second-hand but the Silver Cross pram with large wheels and bouncy springs had a drawback: chalked on the black hood was the message "Almost Perfect - £4 10/–". To my chagrin I was unable to remove these words however much I scrubbed. The new occupant of the pram, born on the 13th November 1956 in the South London Hospital for Women, wasn't almost perfect: he was perfect.

For three or four months John pursued his career as salesman by becoming part of Powerdrive, a small firm manufacturing its own design of sports car. The salary was modest, however, and prospects for promotion limited. He came to the conclusion it made sense to emigrate. For one thing he longed once more to put an ocean between himself and the parents who did not get on with each other and for whom he'd always been pig in the middle. He also shared the feeling of disenchantment pervading Britain after the Suez crisis.

I didn't relish the thought of leaving the home to which I'd become attached but John had made up his mind. He did at least agree to head for London, Ontario, where I'd spent some time during my recent spell in Canada, rather than make for the States.

Zik had by this time adapted well to London. He (or she) had conceived a passion for John's father, hurrying down to the front door each time a fruity cough announced his beloved's arrival. We couldn't take Zik with us, however, and through an advertisement in the Exchange & Mart found him a new owner. This man called round within minutes of the advertisement's appearance, unable to hide his excitement but determined at first to beat us down from the asking price of £30. When he saw the sleek grey parrot with his bright red tail feathers and heard about his repertoire of phrases he peeled off thirty one-pound notes and hurried away with his treasure.

A few days later, on a day when the March sun shone warmly, John, Roderick in his carry-cot and I boarded the Queen Elizabeth for the five-day voyage to New York.

From Grand Central Station we took a train to London, Ontario, where we were met and taken to their home by a young couple I'd got to know three years earlier. Places to rent were as hard to find in this London as in its namesake but with these friends' help we were soon able to move into the top floor of a small house on the outskirts of the town. The bathroom on the ground floor had to be shared with a family of eight. We felt the Dutch landlord and his wife were doing pretty well for themselves but for us there was little choice. For the two rooms and shared plumbing we paid $65 a month.

My parents had lent us £100 to tide us over the first few weeks but it was essential for us both to get work without delay. Jobs were scarce for people without qualifications but John managed to find one as a debt-collector. I signed on at a secretarial agency, spending my first two days typing labels for a juke box. I was glad to leave this deadly occupation to become secretary to the managing director of a small manufacturing firm.

Four-month-old Roderick spent each day with a woman who lived within easy driving distance of our flat. This was just as well since the car we possessed was scarcely roadworthy. Our child-minder was glad of the dollars we paid her since her husband was laid off every winter when during the sub-zero weather the construction industry came to a standstill. Looking after Roderick was not a relaxing business. Ever since we'd arrived in Canada he'd been unable to sleep except for brief snatches either at night or during the day. Our patient minder never complained.

With an abrupt transition from winter to summer the temperature in the two rooms under an uninsulated roof rose to an unendurable level. In May we could stand it no longer. Our baby-minder then told us of a nearby house part of which was normally rented out but which was currently between tenants. We hurried along to this place and were warned by the owner, a large and stately woman with a German accent, that many were after her flat. However her teenage daughter found Roderick so cute she begged her mother to "take the couple with the baby!" Mother agreed to do so.

For a year we enjoyed our new home with its spacious kitchen and our own bathroom. The hot-air heating coming up through the floor-level grills made the whole place cosy during the winter months when outside on the street our eyelashes froze as we waited for the bus to work. We might well have been content if John had been able to find a job to suit him.

But even if he had, London for us would probably never have been a success. We belonged to no particular church and we were embarrassingly hard up. This could have been forgiven if we'd been students but as it was we didn't fit into a respectable category of New Canadian.

If John was depressed before, it was nothing compared with how he felt after developing pneumonia one February afternoon. The intense cold had seeped into him as, wearing an anorak but nothing on his head, he gave the old car a wash. Grey with cold he came inside, to develop a fever that nearly sent the mercury shooting out of the thermometer. Leaving Roderick with our landlady I drove a nearly-collapsing John to the hospital where he was admitted at once.

Home again after a swift recovery John felt he'd failed in Canada; we must return to Britain. But on further reflection he wondered whether perhaps we might not give the States a try. There might perhaps be more opportunities in New York? I knew how little he wanted to go home and the idea of living in that city was exciting.

When we mentioned this plan to our landlady she was withering in her disapproval of a couple who could contemplate abandoning a wholesome existence in Canada for the dubious attractions of New York City.

With the antique desk, oval table and other possessions crated and ready for transmission to the States, John set off at the end of June to look for work and a place to live. Roderick and I stayed behind in a rented room for a few weeks, sweltering in the humid heat of London. So hot did it become that Roderick was invited to spend each night with a kindly Scottish couple recently arrived from Kirkintilloch. Their basement flat may have resembled a dungeon but it was cool and Roderick was able to sleep.

When John had given us the go ahead we set off on the train to join him in New York.

CHAPTER 2

Our apartment in Flushing, Long Island, was the ground floor half of a two-storey building in a complex of new and identical structures. Inside the two rooms, kitchen and bathroom it was even more stiflingly hot than it was outside and as we dumped our cases down I saw that eighteen-month-old Roderick was showing signs of distress. I ran a bath, took his clothes off and put him in the tepid water. Quickly he revived and from then on adapted well to the New York summer.

John and I were exhilarated by the atmosphere of the City. Immigrants from Britain we found were made welcome, which was nice for us, of course, and our English accent was no handicap.

The ability to speak and write fluent French had enabled John to find employment in the Société Générale, a Manhattan bank. I too was accepted straight away to work as one of four secretaries in a non-profit organisation known as The Citizens' Committee for Children of New York, Inc.

We found a child minder by advertising through a local newspaper. Ethel, a black lady from North Carolina, lived on her own with her six-year-old son. For $35 a week she'd collect Roderick each week-day and drive him in her salmon-pink Chevrolet to her house in Jackson Heights, returning him shortly before one or other of us came home from work.

For five months John and I made the long subway journey into our respective offices each day and during this time Roderick was rarely without a feverish cold and cough, picked up from Ethel's schoolboy son. One afternoon in November his suddenly worsened condition alarmed Ethel to such a degree that she drove him to the emergency department of the City Hospital in Queen's County. She telephoned John who then rang me and together he and I sped to the hospital.

In the busy emergency room we found Roderick in good spirits in spite of a high temperature. Thankfully handing him over to us Ethel went off home while a young doctor suggested Roderick might have measles. For this reason he had him admitted into a small private room.

As the new patient was being settled in John and I sat on the edge of our chairs in a corridor to be joined after a little by a hospital chaplain. He sat down beside us and prayed for our little boy's recovery. We were grateful to him but the very fact he was praying seemed to emphasise the gravity of the situation. We were filled with foreboding.

When it became clear the following day that Roderick did not have measles but "a pneumonia", as the nurse put it, he was allowed to stay in his small room instead of being moved to a cot in the children's ward. In spite of being seriously ill for several days he was always cheerful and smiling when we made our daily visits, holding out his arms to be picked up. As we walked back to the car at the end of the visit the nurse carried Roderick to the window so that he could wave goodbye .

We felt that the two weeks of care he received in this City Hospital was as good as any he might have received in a private clinic, and because he'd been admitted as an emergency his hospital stay in cash terms cost us nothing.

Shortly before Christmas when on each corner of every street Santa Claus stood ringing his bell, asking passers-by for donations to charity, my boss gave me the address of a block of apartments in Brooklyn Heights. She knew we'd come to dislike our box-like dwelling in Flushing and from a friend she'd heard of a vacant one-bedroomed apartment. For some reason it hadn't been snapped up in spite of its address. This desirable residential area boasting streets of early nineteenth-century terraced houses overlooked the Hudson River and the Wall Street skyline.

Affordable accommodation was no easier to find in New York during the late 1950s than it had been in Britain; as for a flat situated in an agreeable neighbourhood within easy reach of Manhattan – that was an unrealistic prospect indeed. Nevertheless it appeared that such a place might become ours.

One evening we took the subway to Brooklyn and walked along to Grace Court, a quiet cul de sac. We found the building superintendent who took us to an apartment on the third floor. As soon as he opened the door the reason for the vacancy became evident: an unbelievably dreadful smell. Without crossing the threshold himself our guide explained that an alcoholic had been living there alone with his two Siamese cats and had long since given up any attempt to provide them with lavatory facilities. Venturing into the living-room with handkerchiefs pressed to our noses, we saw that the unfortunate cats had for some time been using the hems of the over-long curtains on which to do their business.

Knowing we'd never get an opportunity like this again we told the superintendent we'd take it. We'd even be paying less since rents in this building could only be increased by a small percentage each time there was a change of tenant and our man had been living there for years. We paid the superintendent his key money, signed the lease and four weeks later when the former tenant and his cats had gone to a private Home we moved in.

Planting Roderick in his cot in the bedroom, mercifully free of any hint of cat, we tackled the source of the smell. With my dressmaking scissors I cut off the hems of the curtains – their good quality made them worth keeping – and stuffed the pieces into a bin-liner, while John ripped up the wall-to-wall carpeting. We then stripped off the wallpaper from the hall and living-room and by supper-time the atmosphere had become tolerable. Many weeks were to pass though before the smell faded completely.

Although Brooklyn was well provided with second-hand furniture shops it didn't stop us from one day taking advantage of a splendid free gift: a double bed in good condition left in the basement for anyone who wanted it. Waiting until few people were about we dragged our find into the lift and up to the apartment.

That night we slept well but woke to find ourselves covered in angry-looking bites. There on the sheet crawled little black insects that could only be bed-bugs. Hoping we'd encounter no-one on the landing, we lugged the infested mattress and base back to the basement, reinstating our old bed, sagging but bug-free.

Fortunately it was Saturday. As soon as the shops were open I hurried to a nearby Puerto Rican hardware store for advice on how to deal with the insects. The salesman produced a can of liquid with which to spray bedding and cracks in walls and floor, endearing himself to me by his assurance that it had worked for him. The chemical was effective; the bugs did not return. Roderick's health improved once we were installed in our new home. While I was at work he was looked after by the building superintendent's wife, Mrs Thacker, a comfortably-built woman in her early 50s. Thanks to her care of Roderick and his obvious contentment at being left in her charge, I lost some of the guilt that nagged at me for leaving my precious child with someone else each day.

From the first, though, it was a thrill to realise we were actually living and working in New York.; wandering along Fifth Avenue in the autumn sunshine I knew what people meant when they claimed there was no limit to what could be accomplished in this city by those with energy and ambition. Of course, along with our English accents it helped in those days that we were white Protestants: "You are the sort of immigrants we want," we were told by one of our neighbours.

There was an ugly side to the brilliance, naturally, but during our two and a half years in this city I personally experienced nothing worse than a bit of molestation on the subway.

The journey from Brooklyn Heights to our respective offices although short could be nasty during the rush-hour when often the trains were packed so tight it was impossible to move away from gropers. One friend told me she always carried a hat-pin in case a man started bothering her; or she would bring down her stiletto heel on the offender's instep. Neither of these remedies appealed to me as I was afraid I'd impale or stamp on the wrong person.

CHAPTER 3

During the months of July and August we could by shutting our eyes imagine ourselves back in the damp heat of Lagos. In the New York dusk people could be seen sitting out on the cast-iron fire escapes snaking down the back of every apartment block, putting off as long as possible a return into their stifling homes. At street level the police braced themselves for the annual surge in 'rumbles' – fights between juvenile gangs.

The Citizens' Committee offices were blessed with nothing to relieve the heat inside the office, not even a fan. The quality of our New York summer nights, however, improved when John brought home a second-hand air conditioner to wedge into the partially-opened window.

Saturday mornings often found us on the subway heading for one of the beaches. Although not the nearest Jones Beach was the cleanest. But it irked having to pay for a hut in which to change. It couldn't be avoided, for anyone seen struggling into a bathing suit under cover of a bath towel risked arrest. An act considered reasonable on a beach in Britain flouted the laws of decency in the State of New York.

The approach of summer sent the Citizens' Committee for Children into high gear. A pressure group whose aim was to improve the lot of children and young people within the State, its professional members comprised two lawyers, an expert in mental health services and the social worker whose secretary I was. The only men who came into our offices were the PhD expert in Protective Services who gave his services to the CCC part-time and a college student earning money during the summer vacation.

The State legislature sat in Albany during the month of May. Its members were bombarded with meticulously-compiled letters from the CCC urging support for the good bills and opposition to the bad. A bill the Committee persuaded the State government to throw out was the one favoured by governments then and now – to make parents punishable for their children's misdeeds. They felt it was doomed to fail. Another of their campaigns aimed at putting a stop to the practice whereby juveniles who'd broken the law were incarcerated in a prison intended for adult offenders and aptly named The Tombs.

My social worker boss devoted much time to the cause of releasing for adoption children who for various bureaucratic reasons were spending their childhood years in a bleak children's home in the City.

The offspring of migrant workers were not forgotten either. Each year these people arrived from other States to spend months working on the land. Housed in hutted camps they were provided with no educational facilities for their children and this state of affairs the CCC was determined should be changed.

The head of our office was a tall woman with a strong German accent and immaculate blonde hair-do. She was the first person I'd known who'd go to Elizabeth Arden merely for a comb-through.

One of the tasks we secretaries had to perform was to take minutes at meetings presided over by our respective bosses. For me this undertaking at which I was never much good anyway was made more difficult by the jargon used. Having got most of the discussions down in shorthand I'd find the notes when transcribed made little sense.

The most efficient of the secretaries was a Negro girl (the word Negro had yet to be superseded by the word Black) with a model's figure. At lunch one day she told me that the ivory shade of her skin was referred to by other Negroes as "high yaller". This colouring had caused her pain rather than satisfaction throughout her life since it was assumed by those with darker skins that she must feel superior to them. Certain white people on the other hand made sure she was aware they were unimpressed by her light colour. She neither wished nor supposed they had been.

The CCC was a good place to work but I longed to spend more time with Roderick who was now three. Middle-class working mothers were not as common in the 1960s as they were to be three decades later and when Roderick asked me why I never fetched him from nursery school as other mothers did I hardly knew what to say.

John's fear that we might be sent home as Distressed British Subjects had by this time receded so he agreed that I should look for part-time work to fit in with the hours Roderick spent at school. Our kind Mrs Thacker had lost her position as building superintendent's wife when her husband died from liver failure and she could no longer be our child minder.

I therefore found a job as secretary and right-hand woman to the owner of a family firm importing leather and plastic from Switzerland for distribution to factories throughout the United States.

Mr Cromwell, German Jewish, wore dark pin-striped suits and pince-nez, liked everything to be just so but was appreciative when one got it right. I loved working for him and in spite of the fact I was only there for three or four hours a day he planned to teach me as much as he could about the business: an exhilarating prospect. I could see myself becoming a person of significance on 34th Street.

Our living arrangements had also improved since we'd been promoted to an apartment affording the luxury of two bedrooms. An even better view of the Hudson River was now ours.

One Saturday morning we stood at the living-room window to watch an Italian cruise ship steaming slowly towards her berth after completing her maiden voyage. The sight of this beauty moving with such majesty, attended by diminutive fire-boats saluting her with vertical jets of water, and the sound of ships' sirens adding their greetings, made speech impossible, so great was the lump in my throat. John was silent too. That winter we were to look out of our window at less elegant ships stuck fast with their cargo in the frozen river.

As a moving-in present Mr Cromwell allowed me to choose a table lamp from a Manhattan store where he enjoyed a discount, while John brought home from his new place of work, a British firm importing furnishing fabrics for the homes of the well-heeled, a roll of glazed chintz for the living-room. In spite of my making them with the flower pattern upside-down the curtains glowed with superior quality.

CHAPTER 4

We were not, however; to enjoy these domestic improvements for much longer. A change in scene was about to overtake us.

"John," asked a former colleague from the Bank, "Why don't you apply for a job with this new UN force that's being sent to the Belgian Congo? On the admin. side they're looking for French-speaking people who've lived in Africa. They say the pay is pretty good."

Much as he enjoyed living in New York City John still hadn't found work to suit him. He also felt that domesticity and the constraints of parenthood had overtaken him too early. Prepared therefore to go off on his own, at least for a while, he presented himself at UN Headquarters. There he was offered a preliminary one-year contract as Administrative Officer in the former Belgian Congo, to take effect from 1st January 1961.

We were both stirred by the knowledge that John was about to join a body of people doing their best to establish order in a situation messy on a grand scale. In other words, it was a cause we could be proud of.

The posting would be to a town named Stanleyville; horror stories about this place had for some months given the papers plenty to write about. No question therefore of wife and child going too. Roderick and I would return to England until or unless it seemed safe to join John.

He wasn't daunted by the possibility of danger. He'd be going to where the action was, where he could make full use of his abilities, where he'd be speaking his beloved French, and also where the per diem allowance for expatriates would boost his salary. In other words our financial prospects had taken an upturn as well.

Plans for departure had to be made swiftly; John would soon be off. At first we both agreed I should stay behind with Roderick for a few weeks and then follow on by sea with our possessions. This would have suited me. Not only could we hang on to things we didn't want to part with but I'd also be able to honour a promise to Mr Cromwell to mind the store during his forthcoming two-week annual visit to Switzerland. Always in a hurry, though, John decided we should all leave by air together. Treasures such as my table lamp and Roderick's mechanical man, Mr Machine, would have to be given away.

Buyers for our furniture were found from within the apartment building. An elderly woman we hadn't met before lowered herself with a sigh of pleasure into the winged armchair she had her eye on. Her smile broadened when we presented her with a footstool to go with it.

In bitter weather we boarded the Boeing. Once inside Roderick asked with deadly clarity,

"Will it crash?"

Two jets had recently collided over Long Island and although we hadn't discussed the disaster within Roderick's hearing, everyone was talking about it.

"No, it won't crash," I assured him as we found our seats. Then I began to feel uneasy, for once airborne the aircraft failed to gain height. Something wasn't right. Suddenly however we were up and away. And over the intercom the captain apologised for the slow ascent, explaining that the severe weather had frozen the undercarriage so that at first it wouldn't retract.

If his explanation was supposed to put our minds at rest it failed with me. Throughout the flight I bit my nails, dreading the moment we came into land at London Airport only to find the undercarriage had stuck again. But of course the temperature in England was many degrees higher than it had been in New York and we landed with all wheels down.

Mary Jean Stewart as Student Nurse, Royal Infirmary, Edinburgh, 1948.

Mary Jean Stewart, Margaret and Tom, 1944.

Naval stores office staff, Trincomalee.

The Wood family emigrates.

Our sitting-room window overlooking the Hudson River.

Roderick with part of football match crowd in Luluabourg.

John on the veranda of our house in Goma with various UN officials and members of the Congolese government in Kivu.

Roderick 'flying' a UN plane.

Interior of DC3 flying between Goma and Leopoldville.

The Woods about to set off on their shopping trip to Elizabethville.

PART V

THE CONGO
1961–1964

CHAPTER 1

John flew to Africa in January 1961 while Roderick.and I settled in for a nice long stay with my parents who were now sharing Desmond's house in Wells-next-the-sea. Desmond, writer and tax exile, was holed up for the winter in his Cairo flat.

The Belgian Congo had become an independent republic in June of the previous year. Little time then elapsed before the Congolese army mutinied, driving out its officers, most of whom were Belgian. Poorly paid, the soldiers felt they were second-class citizens in their own country with little hope of improvement in spite of independence. Resentment in the ranks finally exploded into violence. At the same time, the lid came off long-suppressed tribal animosities; not only Europeans were being attacked but Congolese as well.

Law and order having ceased to exist and with the name "Congo" rapidly becoming synonymous in the world's press with killing and rape, the majority of Belgian settlers fled.

Responding to an appeal from the new Congolese government the United Nations assembled and despatched a peace-keeping force to the vast African country. This force was known in English as the United Nations Operation in the Congo (UNOC) and in French as L'Opération des Nations Unis au Congo (ONUC). Countries who sent contingents included India, Pakistan, Malaya, Indonesia, Eire, Argentina, Norway, Sweden, Nigeria and Ghana.

As well as trying to keep the peace UNOC had to tackle the problem of Katanga. Across the border from Northern Rhodesia, the Province was richly endowed with natural resources such as copper. After South Africa the Belgian Congo was the second richest country in the continent. For the indigenous people and the Belgian settlers Katanga was a good place to be. They liked the way things were and didn't wish to be part of the new republic, obedient to the dictates of the central government in Leopoldville, thank you very much. The provincial Katangese government based in Elizabethville announced its intention to secede.

Naturally, the new government in Leopoldville wasn't having this. The wealth from Katanga must not be hived off for the exclusive benefit of a privileged few in Katanga and the people of Belgium but should be shared by the entire Congolese nation. An armed contingent of the bluebereted force along with political advisers was therefore sent to Elizabethville.

The Belgians hadn't done a good job of training the Congolese to take over positions of responsibility even when they knew independence was inevitable. Consequently, with the departure of the settlers the country was left with neither civil servants nor doctors or technicians of any kind. The UN had to fill this gap.

The technical assistants they recruited had to be housed and supplied with transport, local labour and every sort of back-up to enable them to carry out their tasks. It was to join the band of Administrative Officers in charge of such practical details that John was flying off to Leopoldville in January.

Reporting at Le Royal, the apartment building taken over as UN headquarters, John was pleased to hear that instead of Stanleyville, Luluabourg in Kasai province was to be his destination. This town's main reason for being was as a railway junction in the centre of the Congo.

Meanwhile in England the papers continued to print atrocity stories from the newly-independent country, giving the impression that there wasn't a safe square inch in the whole land.

Luluabourg itself wasn't too bad, however, John told me in his letters, although the assassination of prime Minister Patrice Lumumba in February 1961 had aroused the fury of his supporters in Kasai; two Belgians enjoying their beer on a hotel verandah the evening the news had broken were shot dead by passing soldiers for displaying a lack of respect. Nevertheless, by the month of May John felt the time had come for Roderick and me to join him. The press, he pointed out, naturally picked on anything sensational but life in Luluabourg was jogging along more or less normally and he'd like us to join him. Not entirely reassured by this optimistic point of view, I realised the UN wouldn't allow wives and children to go out there if too much risk were involved.

John wrote of the villa he'd taken over: a roomy one-storey building with generous verandah and garden. One of many situated within a large and pleasantly laid-out housing estate it had until Independence belonged to a Belgian family. (John told me later that the UN political adviser stationed in Luluabourg objected to the Admin. Officer's decision to take over this complex of houses instead of accommodation in the town itself. He argued that it betrayed a regrettable lack of trust in the Congolese; how much more diplomatic to have commandeered houses with Congolese neighbours, instead of distancing himself and UN personnel by a matter of several kilometres. Several months later John's more realistic attitude over this issue was vindicated.)

Off to the Norfolk and Norwich Hospital Roderick and I went for injections, including the one against Yellow Fever. Roderick suffered the painful jab with stoicism, causing the doctor to remark that he was the best boy she had ever given an injection to. Several times that evening I heard him saying to himself "The best boy": her words had pleased him.

We flew to Leopoldville at the end of May, John meeting us at the airport. Before being allowed to leave the plane, however, we had to wait while an airport employee came on board to spray the inside of the cabin with DDT. The object of this suffocating exercise was not explained.

Driving along 40km of straight, featureless road leading to the city we overtook Congolese walking long distances to their places of work in the capital. When we reached it Leopoldville proved to be large, with many trees lining the wide boulevards. Imposing government buildings exuded melancholy in their emptiness. Shops still traded but, I was later to discover, boasted minimal stocks, especially of day-to-day objects. Although possible to buy a dress copied from a Vogue design and made on the premises of a boutique, it wasn't so easy to find an egg-beater or a tyre for the car.

Our hotel for two nights was large and modern, the room fairly clean, the staff dour. We ate breakfast of rolls and apricot jam, with bitter coffee for John and me, Fanta orange for Roderick. After the long flight, with an over-excited four-year-old to try to calm down in the sweat-inducing heat, the sound of the wrought-iron chairs screeching over the gritty paved terrace every time someone moved set my teeth on edge.

Next day we were taken by a young American Admin Officer to the university campus. Classes had ceased with the onset of independence but the open-air swimming pool made a focal point on hot afternoons for UN personnel and other expatriates.

As we relaxed in our bathing suits at the water's edge John mentioned we were leaving in the morning for Luluabourg. A British journalist sitting near us exclaimed "Is it safe?" A tactless question, I considered, and one that had been lurking at the back of my mind.

CHAPTER 2

We took off from Leo in a DC3 packed with assorted UN personnel, military and civilian, returning from a break in the capital. As we approached our destination the town seemed from the air to be surrounded by nothing but a sea of woolly-looking bush, obviously not a place to have to make a forced landing in. It shocked but did not surprise me when John remarked,

"It's cannibal country down there".

Driving through gates guarded by Nigerian soldiers we drew up at a long, low bungalaw with red-tiled roof. Dusty, unpaved roadways criss-crossing the estate led to other houses, mostly empty, their once well-manicured gardens now overgrown. Trees of no particular distinction did their best to relieve the flatness of the terrain, as did the reds and yellows of shrubs familiar to me from my Ceylon experience. When the engine of our American four-wheel drive cut out, the metallic clicking of invisible cicadas provided a noisy background of sound as the heat enveloped us.

Looking around me I was then struck by the fact that the housing estate described by John as being "surrounded by barbed wire" was meagrely protected; one well-aimed kick at the wire fencing would surely flatten it. I noticed also that half our garden lay inside and half outside the barricade of coiled barbed wire. But still, it was reassuring to be told our nearest neighbours were British officers attached to The Queen's Own Nigerian Regiment and some yards away I could see the roofs of tents where the troops were encamped.

Apart from the military our only other neighbours consisted of a French Canadian couple working for the Red Cross and a young Portugese who with his wife had converted one of the villas into a UN guest house.

In the middle of the grass in front of our house stood an empty aviary; near it a large and spiteful-looking cactus stuck out its pointed leaves. The deep verandah at one end of the building, however, drew us into its shade and there we were greeted by members of local staff recruited by John to help him with the administrative work. Here also Roderick received the first of many head-pattings. Italians especially couldn't resist giving his blonde hair a stroke.

A stocky Milanese, moustachioed face creasing into a smile, shook hands and showed me with pride the saucepans he'd arranged to buy for our kitchen. Not knowing that to find anything of this nature in the local shops represented a coup, I mentally turned my nose up at the tinny quality of the pans. John then introduced me to Jerome the cook. Tall and unsmiling Jerome spoke fluent French. Mine had never progressed beyond School Certificate standard so that although equipped with a good grasp of the past historic, I was going to have to learn from this Congolese the French for everyday objects such as oven, floorcloth, sandwich and gas cylinder.

Roderick spent each morning at a primary school run by the Sisters of a Roman Catholic order. Some of these women had been roughly treated at the time of Independence but had refused to leave the country.

Each morning after I'd dropped him off, I'd see our small boy sitting at the feet of Ma Soeur, the Sister who sat on an upright chair supervising the children's arrival.

Being plunged into a school where most of the children were Congolese and where no one else spoke English cannot have been much fun. And in the afternoons he had only me to keep him company although for a while a small boy called Medard appeared from beyond the fence to join Roderick on the verandah. Aged six or seven he was smaller in stature than Roderick; he fitted perfectly into a pair of outgrown Ladybird pyjamas whose bright red colour complemented the darkness of his skin. But then Medard stopped coming. He'd been taken up as a sort of mascot by a Scandinavian helicopter crew living in a nearby villa. Anyway, life was much too serious a matter for him to be able to enter into the spirit of childish games with a four-year-old 'blanc'.

Each day the fresh brilliance of the mornings inspired in me a feeling of optimism. I wrote letters or dress-made while Jerome and his assistant bustled about the house cleaning, doing our laundry and preparing the lunch. In other words, something was going on. But by late morning the heat had clamped down and then up loomed the endless afternoon.

Dashing home at lunch time, John would be off again by one o'clock, not returning until six at the earliest. One hour could be disposed of while Roderick and I had a rest. Then as my clock struck two I'd call out "You can get up now!" A thud followed by the patter of bare feet and the arrival of a small boy in my room indicated Roderick's readiness to start whatever it was we'd do for the next four hours.

We played records John had bought in a Luluabourg shop in the process of closing down. Most of these records were of classical works but there was one that wasn't and Roderick never tired of it: a recording by Les Pompiers, an American group, singing hits from the 20s and 30s. Every afternoon we listened to "If you knew Susie like I knew Susie" followed by something that ended with the words ".....last night on the back porch I loved her most of all". We came to know them backwards.

Backwards also did we come to know the text of Beatrix Potter's "Jeremy Fisher", one of the few books we'd been able to bring with us. Roderick also liked the aeroplane I made out of cotton reels, sticks and string. We could go for walks around the estate, of course, but the silence was unnerving. Everyone except us took long siestas lasting right through to early evening. There were some, however, who stayed awake: our neighbours the British army officers. They invited Roderick and me to drop in for tea whenever we were passing.

That their peace-keeping role in the Congo didn't fill them with enthusiasm was plain. On one of our visits a young officer, shocked by the horrors he'd seen in another part of the Congo, claimed half-jokingly to be considering getting himself sent back to the UK with a nervous breakdown.

For Roderick and me the afternoons picked up when John found a jeep for me to use. A mile or two out of town was a former Belgian club with swimming pool. The water was green and opaque but fine for cooling off in as long as you kept your mouth shut. Naturally there'd be no one else about between two and six o'clock, except for the Congolese barman who materialised when it was time for Roderick and me to have our drink of Fanta orange. My fluency in French still hadn't progressed much; stilted banalities were all I could produce in the way of conversation.

"Ça va?"

"Oui, ça va."

Occasionally a group of Congolese children brought life and noise to the club premises. With no one to tell them not to they'd run up to the edge of the pool and plunge in, clothes and all, splashing about in what had until recently been forbidden territory.

As the year wore on, if Roderick and I prolonged our stay at the club until tea-time we'd be joined by the family of John's expatriate Italian colleague. Josie, mother of two young boys, made sure that at least four hours passed between their eating lunch and venturing into the water. According to her they'd sink like stones if the gap were any less.

Josie couldn't hide her disapproval of the long, wide-legged shorts in the style favoured by British colonials I'd bought for Roderick. (It is true they were not flattering to thin, childish legs.) She also fretted over her house-boy's inability to keep her flat spotless, fighting a losing battle in the kitchen against the ants. But she was proud of the fact she'd been one of the first UN wives to join their husbands in the former Belgian Congo after Independence.

The modern hospital in Luluabourg was staffed by a contingent of the Indian Army Medical Corps. The officers made us welcome in their Mess and invited us to their film shows. To distinguish them from Cowboys-and-Indians-Indians Roderick referred to these kindly people as Indian-Mess-Indians .

While waiting one evening for 'The Brides of Dracula' to start up, I found myself sitting next to an Ethiopian army officer, a handsome man he was with dark brown skin, fine features and serious expression. During our conversation he told me with sadness that divorces among UN personnel were exceeded in number only by those in Hollywood. The film began before I could find out what had prompted this remark, but at any rate I thought smugly divorce was something that would never affect John and me.

A young British captain who'd undoubtedly been in the thick of some dangerous happenings during his time in the Congo had decided not to come to the cinema that evening. He knew he'd find the film too frightening. Parts of it were indeed terrifying. I went to bed later convinced I'd be unable to sleep.

Having dropped off with no trouble, I was yanked awake in the small hours by a scream from Roderick. (He hadn't been to the film, of course.) Leaping out of bed and rushing along the passage I found him sitting up and gazing with fear at some object in the corner of the room. The cause of his fright turned out to be a large moth. This was quickly disposed of but when I put my arms round him I couldn't at first utter a word of reassurance since my Dracula-influenced terror was making my jaw wobble up and down in an extraordinary way.

CHAPTER 3

The Brigadier in charge of the Nigerian contingent asked me one day if I'd like to do secretarial work for him. He was a man respected by the Congolese as well as by his own officers and I liked the idea of working for him. It would be good also to earn some francs. The work wasn't demanding: official letters and confidential reports on his staff to write, and weekly attendance with my notebook at Morning Prayers when officers, British and Congolese, delivered their reports.

One day when there was no work to be done, I accompanied the Brigadier and a Ghanaian general on a visit to Leopoldville in the Force Commander's plane. While they attended to matters of state I'd get in a day's shopping. When we landed at Leo a ladder was propped up against the side of the aircraft. The two men descended first, politely waiting at the foot for me to join them. The perpendicular angle at which the ladder was standing made it advisable to go down slowly and with care. About half-way I became impatient and decided to jump the last few feet. This I did with no trouble except that the hem of my skirt caught on the top of the ladder. As my feet hit the tarmac my skirt remained in the air. Scrambling up a few rungs, I managed to unhitch the material and this time descended to the bottom of the ladder one step at a time. When I saw my companions' embarrassment at this inelegant spectacle I suppressed the desire to burst out laughing. And as we walked to the awaiting car with its little flag on the bonnet I silently thanked the Good Lord that my skirt had been made of tough Horrockses cotton, not easily torn.

Having purchased our weekly treat of imported steak from the Belgian-owned butcher's shop – "de la viande" the manageress gently corrected me when I baldly asked for "viande, s'il vous plais", I decided to call in at the ironmonger's. Who knows, they might have something useful to buy. When the Flemish shopkeeper realised I was British he swept me upstairs to his flat to meet his English wife. With introductions made he returned to keep an eye on his African assistant.

The young woman, thin and anxious-looking, shook hands before hurrying through to the kitchen to fetch the coffee. She placed a cup on the table beside me, spilling some of the liquid as she did so. Then hunched on the edge of her chair she poured out her fears.

At home in Luluabourg at the time of independence she'd witnessed such scenes of brutality as to unnerve her completely. Although she hadn't been harmed she couldn't rid herself of images of rape and beatings. A particularly distressing memory concerned a friend of hers who'd been raped by several soldiers while her children hid a few feet away in the garage roof. Dreading that these horrors might happen again, this sad person was desperate to leave the Congo. However, her husband wouldn't hear of it.

Unable to think of anything encouraging to say since by this time my stomach was knotted up with dread, I left her. A promise to visit her again wasn't to be kept since before many weeks were up she herself was to become a victim of rape. This time her desire to get away was no longer thwarted by her husband.

Shortly after this meeting I talked to a young Pole, also married to a Belgian. Having herself personally witnessed no brutal acts, her nerves were still intact and she was able to tell stories of 'incidents' with humour.

Shortly after Independence Congolese troops converged on Leopoldville; a Belgian woman living on her own sat waiting. As soon as the first few soldiers approached, she went outside onto the street. She accosted a sturdily-built man wearing the insignia of sergeant and told him if he'd look after her, protecting her from the others, she would be his woman. He said he would, and moved into her house.

For several weeks he made certain she came to no harm until the day arrived for her evacuation. Then, solicitous to the last, he escorted her to the airport, helped her into the plane packed with women and children, and waved goodbye with some sadness as she flew away towards Brussels.

Another person with courage and presence of mind, my Polish friend continued, was sitting on her own one evening when in burst a Congolese soldier. He announced he was going to rape her.

"Oh, you can't do that. I've had an operation and there's nothing left."

She then showed him her hysterectomy scar. He accepted her objection as being reasonable, asked for a photograph instead and took his leave.

A locally-recruited member of staff working for John had also survived the 'evenements' of 1960. He and his family were settlers of long standing in the Congo and with his contacts Medardo was able to give much practical help to the Admin Officer.

Maria his wife possessed the combined talents of haute couture dressmaker and superlative cook. Because of the ugly turn of events during the previous year they'd packed off their three older children to the grandparents in Italy, keeping two-year-old Katia with them. Although she missed her children acutely Maria was always cheerful and invitations to her Sunday lunches were received with pleasure by the British officers as well as by the Wood family. Food was not plentiful in Luluabourg and Maria's pasta dishes, made with eggs from her chickens, afforded us all a treat.

As Admin Officer John had access to the UN commissary. Amongst its limited stocks could be found seven-pound tins of tomatoes, peaches and mixed fruit salad, all of which appeared regularly on our menu. Fortunately for us, however, Jerome was expert at making the soups favoured by the Belgians. These made good starters to meals of flavourless steak, chips and salad of limp lettuce. This uninspired menu was what the American ambassador to the Congo was offered when one evening he and his aide came to dinner with us. The Belgian ambassador was later similarly treated when he visited Luluabourg, but in spite of the dull food and obvious lack of trouble taken by the Admin Officer's wife who was by this time suffering from a serious lack of enthusiasm for life in Luluabourg, both evenings passed in an atmosphere of conviviality. There was, of course, no lack of duty-free drink to jolly things along.

The two main tribes in Kasai Province were the Luluas and the Balubas. These people didn't get on; fighting in the bush frequently broke out between them. One afternoon I was startled when a jeep screeched up to our villa, the Army captain at the wheel braking violently in a cloud of dust. John jumped out, shouting to me as he dashed inside,

"If shooting starts you and Roderick must go into the store-room".

(This small space between dining-room and kitchen was windowless).

"What shooting?"

But John had already collected up what he'd come for and was being driven away at speed, presumably to go and check on hostilities.

Wondering what I could do to prepare for a possible attack, I was relieved when in walked a friend of ours, a Pakistani major.

"What's all the panic about?" Mike asked.

"I've no idea. But would you like a drink?"

In spite of the fact that it was only two o'clock in the afternoon, he agreed that to have a stiff drink was a sensible move. We might as well lay in Dutch courage for whatever might transpire.

Drinking gin and tonic while Roderick played with his home-made aeroplane, we waited. Nothing happened. The fighting had evidently fizzled out.

The two tribes tried to make it up a few months later when their leaders organised a meeting of reconciliation in Luluabourg. President Kasavubu had been invited, and John in his official capacity had been asked to attend. I went too since John felt it would be civil to bring his wife.

We found the reception hall crowded with earnest-looking black men in European suits and sad-looking cardboardy shoes. There were no other white women present but seated modestly at the back of the room were the participants' spouses. Their vividly-coloured dresses brightened the scene. I sat down next to them although we couldn't converse since they spoke no French and I no Lingala, but we exchanged smiles and amiable gestures. John had meanwhile taken his place with the men.

Shifting from one side of my behind to the other to avoid cramp while the speeches droned on, I happened to catch President Kasavubu's eye. As he graciously raised his glass of non-alcoholic drink in my direction he was I was sure indicating admiration for the shocking pink Vogue dress run up for me by Maria.

CHAPTER 4

With these various excitements behind him and feeling in need of a break after eight months of Luluabourg, John decided to take a holiday. We'd escape for ten days from the gloom of the Congo to Dar es Salaam on the east coast of the British colony Tanganyika. Travel costs would be modest since we could fly for nothing in a UN plane as far as Albertville, then cross Lake Tanganyika by boat to Kigoma. From there we'd catch a train to the coast.

The journey was long but without incident Roderick, however, underwent an experience that while it lasted caused him dreadful anxiety and about which I suffered equally dreadful remorse when some years later he spelt it all out.

During the flight to Albertville the pilot asked our four-year-old if he'd like to fly the plane. John escorted him up to the cockpit where he sat in front of the controls, not daring to let go of the wheel for an instant since as he was driving the plane it would no doubt instantly crash if he did. Who finally released him from his ordeal I can't remember, but it was no thanks to any sensitivity on our part.

Arriving at last in Dar es Salaam we booked into a hotel not far from the beach. My spirits rose. Ideal for buckets and spades, the beach was studded with rocks to clamber on, while at the foot of the cliffs dark caves invited exploration. For a week our days were spent in and out of the sea, our bodies warmed by a benevolent sun. The sun in Luluabourg was not for sitting out in. (I'd been told that not long ago it had killed a Belgian woman who'd done some before-lunch gardening when the sun was at its most powerful).

The English proprietor and his wife were welcoming, the African staff friendly. Black people we passed on our way to the beach next morning called out "Jambo!" (Swahili greeting) or, in equally cheerful manner, "Uhuru!", meaning "Freedom!".

Making sand castles with moats down to the water one afternoon we were joined by a Frenchman, elegant in silk shirt and well-pressed linen trousers. An expert in engineering (there were many 'experts' in UNOC), he urged John to include Zanzibar in the holiday itinerary. Visiting that island was a cultural experience we could not afford to miss.

Culture be blowed. Roderick and I were having a lovely, undemanding, anxiety-free seaside holiday and we were happy to stay put. However, John was persuaded by this Frenchman's enthusiasm for two compelling reasons: first, he wasn't all that keen on the image of Mum-Dad-and-the-Kid-at-the-seaside; and second, he couldn't think of a reason that would convince this suave bachelor of the necessity for staying where we were. We set off for Zanzibar without delay.

A short crossing by motor boat took us to the island. Certainly the old city built by the Arabs to process the slave traffic was picturesque with its narrow streets and heavy, magnificently carved studded wooden doors.

Booked into a hotel we then hired a car to drive round the island -

green and full of dense undergrowth. We saw the house in which Dr Livingstone had for a time lived and we ended up having lunch with the British Consul and his wife.

Zanzibar didn't keep us for long, however, since John was eager to fit in a visit to Elizabethville before our return to Luluabourg. He wanted to see this part of the Congo that was evidently managing to function in normal fashion, even though the problem caused by the Katangese determination to secede had still not been solved; in fact, there had been several evenements in Elizabethville during the past year. But the combination of shops full of imported goods and a splendid climate beckoned. To me also there was a sombreness in the atmosphere of Zanzibar that reminded me too much of gloomy Congo. I therefore welcomed the suggestion of a trip to Elizabethville.

Returning to Albertville by the way we'd come, we took off for Elizabethville in a DC4 crewed by Argentinians.

Once airborne the aircraft bucketed about in the turbulence. This was unfortunate since something I'd eaten was making my stomach feel odd. With no warning I was tremendously sick, erupting like a geyser, to the discomfiture of John, Roderick and two passengers sitting near us. A member of the crew put a camp bed in the aisle for me to lie on and this helped calm my insides but the cold seeping up through the canvas made it impossible to stop shivering. However, as soon as we started the descent I felt better. And in the cramped lavatory smelling as though it hadn't been attended to for weeks I struggled into a clean dress .

Disembarking at Elizabethville Airport we noticed as we crossed the tarmac the UN soldiers were out in force. Something must be up, particularly as officers were wearing revolvers, something I hadn't noticed before. Since UNOC was a peace-keeping force its weapons only appeared when a crisis blew up.

A blue-turbaned Sikh officer, tall and handsome with beard neatly tucked into hairnet, spoke to John.

"I think you should take your lady wife back to Albertville on the next flight."

The atmosphere in Elizabethville was, he told us, extremely tense. John disliked being told what to do when he'd already decided on a particular course of action, and there were plenty of others prepared to set off into town. We would therefore proceed as planned. With diminished enthusiasm I waited with Roderick while transport into town was organised for us.

Three young Norwegians also on their way to Elizabethville were happy for the three of us to squeeze into the back of their small white car with the UN emblem on its side. Squashed together in the front there was little space for the automatic weapon one of them was holding.

With some miles still to go before the city was reached we could see ahead to where a crowd of Congolese were standing along the edges of a roundabout; they appeared to be waiting for someone or something. A minute or two later we discovered what. Shrieking the word "ONI!" (their way of pronouncing ONU) the waiting men let fly with vicious accuracy a barrage of stones and rocks at this hated symbol of UN oppression – our car.

Enjoying a ring-side view some white women could be observed leaning over garden gates, homely in aprons and slippers, craning their necks so as to get a closer look at the action.

Windscreen and front windows of the car were smashed. The fusillade went on forever.

"We are going to be killed! Please God let it be quick, with with no mucking about."

No doubt others were sending up similar SOS's to the Almighty and meanwhile our driver kept going.

With blood streaming from cuts in his face he kept his hands on the wheel and foot on the accelerator. Like a World War II merchant ship avoiding U-boats he zigzagged this way and that. The young man sitting next to him, also bleeding from facial cuts, held his weapon high as though about to use it. He couldn't fire it, though. He was too firmly hemmed in on both sides. If I could have helped him in some way to shoot at these people I would have done so. We were in mortal danger and the instinct for self-preservation was uppermost.

Suddenly, unbelievably, we were through. Having run the gauntlet for an eternity (minutes at most) we were tearing along an empty road. Our driver must have felt it wasn't possible we'd escaped our attackers: they had to be chasing us. They weren't of course since they had no vehicles but we sped along as though the devil were after us, at some point crossing the border into Northern Rhodesia. Until we reached a quiet cluster of houses that included a government Guest House, no one said a word.

During the attack John had pushed Roderick's head down onto his lap, while I, feeling craven, hid my head behind John's back. We both hoped our five-year-old wouldn't have realised the danger we'd been in. (He told us years later that he hadn't been taken in by the remarks we'd made about those "naughty men throwing stones at the car").

Apart from being frightened I'd been shocked by my first experience of anti-UN feeling. The sight of the uniform topped by beret or forage cap in a cheerful shade of blue appeared to inspire respect in Luluabourg: we UN civilians were definitely on the side of the good guys. Some Katangese with their Belgian chums had, however, made plain their hatred for the interfering UN presence.

On the radio next morning we heard that this demonstration was just one of many carried out in or near Elizabethville that day. A much graver incident it would undoubtedly have been if our Norwegian had succeeded in firing his weapon.

With the one-day protest over, no disturbances interrupted our drive back to the airport. There we joined a flight to Albertville and a few hours later were in Luluabourg.

I don't know who was the more upset, Roderick or I, when we discovered our beautiful, affectionate cat, given to Roderick by the Indians, had disappeared. He had probably been eaten.

CHAPTER 5

The streets of Luluabourg may have been calm but the presence of 5,000 ANC (Armee Nationale Congolaise) soldiers camped on the outskirts of town did little for one's peace of mind. However, although their morale was low and their mood uncertain they were not regarded as a serious threat. "They couldn't organise a Sunday school picnic" was John's comforting opinion.

The Congolese military police known as the Gendarmerie were something else. They enjoyed throwing their weight about and beating people up for the hell of it. One November night they turned very nasty indeed. Out on on the rampage they arrested many anciens, (the name given to long-established Europeans), raping the wives of several. The latter victims I heard later included the unhappy young woman from the flat over the shop.

Jerome brought news of these happenings when he arrived for work.

He was soon followed into the camp by Belgian women seeking sanctuary with their children in the comparative security of the (partially) barbed-wire-enclosed housing estate. Some of their menfolk had been seized by the Gendarmerie and the women were sick with worry.

Maria and three-year-old Katia we welcomed into our house; Maria's husband had also been rounded up and she dreaded to think what might be happening to him. (He was in fact unharmed).

Roderick was pleased to have the little girl's company since we were all confined to the house and to give herself something to do Maria helped me embroider a six-foot-long tablecloth I'd started on a month or two previously. Her stitching was so shaky I unpicked it all when the crisis was past.

(Years later I regretted having done this. Maria's contribution would have remained a graphic reminder of the frightening episode).

When the dust had settled and all the Europeans had been released, the Brigadier held an emergency meeting with his staff. Three senior Congolese army officers attended. The Brigadier's manner reminded me of a headmaster berating his pupils for some grave misdemeanour, although in this case it was dejected-looking men who sat with heads lowered and shoulders drooping. They had little to say when the Brigadier expressed his disgust over the disgraceful behaviour of the Gendarmerie.

Normality returned to Luluabourg as abruptly as it had departed. Families returned to their homes in the town although Roderick's school stayed shut and he and I continued to be confined to barracks.

During the day there were Nigerian soldiers to chat to. One NCO in particular liked to talk to Roderick, bringing him a present of a pair of white sneakers. He then announced he'd like to take the two of us back to Nigeria with him.

Deciding to take refuge in a girl-guidey voice I gushed:

"Gosh, that's nice of you, but I honestly don't think my husband would like it."

The subject was dropped.

Surfacing one afternoon, Roderick and I discovered our Nigerian friends in the process of making a barricade of sandbags on the verandah. Within it crouched a machine gun.

"What's all this for?"

"It's for your protection, Madam."

Thanks for providing the ANC with a worthwhile target, I thought but didn't say.

By this time John was working longer hours than ever; the lack of companionship for Roderick and me during the day was getting me down. I therefore suggested to John that since his contract expired at the end of December and it was now late November, would it not be a good idea for Roderick and me to leave soon and go home for Christmas? John agreed.

The morning of our departure from Luluabourg Maria came to say goodbye. She told me that at the time of the recent unpleasantness friends of hers had taken comfort from the fact that Madame Wood had not immediately packed her bags and flown off with Roderick to safety. They'd construed from this that the situation was perhaps not as serious as they'd feared.

Maria's remark made me to feel like a character from the Girls' Own Paper – stiff upper lip and all that. (Could we have got out? I doubted it). Anyway, knowing that our housing estate was several miles from town and with the Nigerian battalion providing a comforting shield, I'd never felt we were in any real danger. What had become hard to endure was the loneliness.

Two weeks before Christmas John put Roderick and me onto the North Star, a DC8 belonging to the UN. Crewed by Canadians the North Star flew regularly between Leo and Europe.

Passengers were not spoilt: they sat on metal seats ranged along the bulkheads and because there was no pressurisation the noise was deafening once we were airborne. Earmuffs were given out, but Roderick and I didn't have to put up for long with the double discomfort of noise and hard seats. As the only woman and child aboard we were invited forward into the crew's section. This was pressurised.

The small compartment behind the cockpit contained a bunk on which crew members normally took it in turns to have a lie down. This was generously offered to Roderick and me with a warning to watch out during the night in case Roderick's finger-tips started to turn blue. If this happened he must be given some oxygen.

Roderick slept soundly and in the cramped space it was a job to get at his fingers to see what colour they were. As far as I could tell they stayed pink.

The long journey came to an end at midnight when we touched down at Pisa. From the airport we were driven to the hotel where John had booked us a room, and after a meal of soup thick enough to stand a spoon up in, we went to bed.

Woken at six o'clock by the clanging of church bells and the buzzing of my alarm clock Roderick announced with satisfaction,

"That was a good sleep."

Twelve hours later the lift took us up to our room in the Great Eastern Hotel, Liverpool Street, Roderick so tired by this time that I had to carry him. The sombre, old-fashioned room to which tea and ham sandwiches were brought by a maid in cap and apron, was profoundly comforting.

CHAPTER 6

Money had been tight during our two and a half years in New York. For example, the summer before we left for Africa John blew his top when I upset the weekly budget by spending 98 cents on a pair of rubber sandals I could have managed without. However, at the completion of his first year as an international civil servant we were beginning to enjoy a certain loosening of the stays, financially speaking. We celebrated by taking a two-week skiing holiday in Austria .

Contributing towards the healthier bank balance was the per diem allowance made to UN expatriates in the field. This money went a long way towards covering day-to-day expenses and left almost untouched the salary paid in dollars into John's bank account. There were also two exchange rates for Congolese francs: official and unofficial. For us the unofficial rate was advantageous indeed.

Invigorated by the holiday in Austria, we were delighted to learn when John reported for duty at Le Royal that his next posting was to be to the small town of Goma. This desirable spot in the eastern province of Kivu, situated at an altitude of several thousand feet, was blessed with a splendid climate and richly-productive soil.

The sun sparkled on Lake Kivu as we arrived at a small house on the hill overlooking the town of Goma. The owner of this house was a Belgian baroness who lived nearby in another of her properties. However, in spite of views of lakes, hills and still–active volcano, all of which we felt compelled to photograph constantly, we were pleased when a large house on the shores of Lake Kivu became available.

Spacious and cool, this house was separated from the lake by lawns, small trees and shrubs; at the back was a courtyard dominated by eucalyptus trees. Sufficiently imposing to have served as an embassy our new home contained three large bedrooms, dining area that led through an archway to the verandah, and a living roon whose open fireplace provided warmth and the smell of wood-smoke on cool evenings .

Down at the lake's edge a small wooden jetty made a convenient meeting place for crown birds whose crests of feathers stood up like 1980s-style Mohican hairdo's.

The UN military contingent based in Goma was from Malaya; their commanding officer a British colonel. Some of the men had been billeted in our house for a while and following their departure a colony of red ants had taken up residence in the kitchen. As I entered it for the first time my flesh crawled when I noticed a cluster the size of a bunch of grapes clinging to the bottom of the fridge. One of the ants broke away and sank its little fangs into my ankle. The pain from this one bite reminded me of horror stories wherein red ants on the march devour anything and anyone they meet.

Backing smartly out of the kitchen, I asked one of the Malayans if he'd get rid of the ants. How it was done I didn't hang around to find out – there was something obscene about this glistening red mass – but gone they were the next time I put my head round the door.

Mosquitoes invaded the house that first night although we'd been assured of their eradication in this part of Goma. John and I weren't bitten but Roderick woke in the morning with face and arms covered in bites. The bedroom windows were all well screened but we found at the end of a passage near his room a small window with broken glass panes. Finding their way through this handy aperture the mosquitoes had made for the nearest human being.

John sought out the local mosquito exterminator who arrived in due course with a DDT spray strapped to his back. Together he and I searched the grounds for the probable breeding place. We soon found it in rough grass at the side of the house: an upturned dustbin lid containing water thick with larvae. A burst of DDT before the lid was emptied ensured that Roderick suffered no more bites.

A volcano smouldered away some miles from Goma. At night we were reminded of its still-active state by the red glow emerging from its summit. In fact only a few years previously it had erupted although the flow of lava by-passed the nearby villages, hissing instead into the lake.

Kivu's soil produced many crops, my favourite being the miniature banana; no other banana I've eaten possesses that sweet but tangy flavour. Locally-grown strawberries and artichokes also appeared frequently on our table. (We came to realise that the many French acquaintances who invited themselves to stay had done so partly because of the artichokes – a tedious vegetable until one reached the centre). Across the border in Ruanda Burundi the lake was well stocked with telapia; the flavour of this fish was so delectable we couldn't get enough of it. As for the locally-grown coffee: patient Elias was kept on the hop by our repeated cries of "Two cups of coffee, please!" An Irish woman living in Goma was even more addicted to this drink, eventually having to be treated for caffeine poisoning.

CHAPTER 7

After Independence many Congolese working for Belgian families had lost their jobs. It hadn't been difficult therefore for John to find well-trained servants. Joseph in his fifties, skin the colour of ebony, wore a red fez and a green apron over his white shirt and khaki trousers. He had an endearing chuckle, sounding as though he'd seen it all and wasn't going to be surprised by anything.

Joseph's former employer had taught him what must have been the abstract art of haute cuisine. Although always ready to finish off anything we hadn't consumed at supper, Joseph and Elias would settle down afterwards to a proper meal based on manioc.

Elias who did the housework was a gentle person who never seemed to mind how much ironing he had to do and he did it brilliantly. He spoke Swahili more easily than French, not that Swahili was his mother-tongue but it was the lingua franca in those parts. With the help of a colonial-style grammar book John and I learnt as much Swahili as we could, skipping such phrases as "Boy! Draw my bath" and "What have you done with Madam's curling tongs?"

When he joined our household Elias moved into one of a pair of concrete garages at the back of the house; divided into two rooms by a curtain it made a snug home for him and his wife. The thud of manioc being pounded in a heavy wooden basin was the only sound his wife ever seemed to make and we hardly saw her. But every now and then she'd sidle up to the back door to ask for a few bottles of cold beer with which to entertain guests: such a reasonable request could not be refused.

European families who'd left Goma after the horrors of 1960 were starting to return. A small primary school run on Belgian lines was opened and amongst its new pupils was Roderick. One of the books he brought home was a reading primer up to whose level I was thankful he never got. (We departed from Goma before his class reached that stage). The book contained the drawing of a woman, framed in black. Across one corner of the picture was a swathe of black material. The caption underneath read: "Remi has lost his mother. Remi reveres his mother." The author must have considered it salutary for children to realise their mothers were not immortal but could die just like anyone else.

The curriculum of this school had got stuck somewhere in the 1930s. Nevertheless its old-fashioned ways pleased the parents with its sense of order and security. Smiles lit up black, brown and white faces as parents fetched their children at the end of the first day.

"Äa commence!" exclaimed a shopkeeper to no one in particular as he waited for his son. The young pupils came from Congolese, Asian and European families, some of them English-speaking. This made a pleasant change for Roderick.

Life for the three of us in Goma was indeed proving to be far more agreeable than it had been in glum Luluabourg. The sunshine could be enjoyed not avoided, even during the wet season when punctually every afternoon clouds the colour of ink loomed up, crashing together to produce thunder, lightning and torrents of rain. The storms were quickly over, however, and out would come the sun once more.

We, our lake-side neighbours and frequent visitors spent much time sun-bathing or swimming. Unlike other stretches of water in Africa, Lake Kivu was free of bilharzia. We could swim without fear of catching the disease.

Roderick was given a guinea-pig, a large, glossy creature whom he named Jeannie. He also acquired a 'tortoise', for which we paid 100 francs, but there was something wrong with the creature. He or she wouldn't eat, just huddled looking miserable. Thinking it might enjoy a paddle we carried it to the lake-side. Lunging into the water the tortoise stuck its head under the surface and kept it there. This must have been what the poor thing, obviously a terrapin, had been desperate for.

Our next-door neighbours, a young couple from France, occupied a one-storey wooden summer house on the lake shore. The annexe to this dwelling was home to John's secretary, a Manchester girl with a gentle manner and the ability to speak fluent French. Another welcome English-speaking visitor to our house was Kurt, meteorologist from West Germany. Over six feet tall he never lost his cool whatever the frustrations at work or in daily living. Even in this Congolese Garden of Eden problems weren't absent for long.

The indigenous population crowded into a village outside the town: no lakeside dwellings for them. The Congolese army also had its presence but relations between its soldiers and the Malayans were amiable, football matches being a regular feature.

The local people had to be wary of the Gendarmerie, however, since they, like their counterparts in Luluabourg, enjoyed being nasty. Our gardener didn't escape their notice. He turned up to work one morning with a bleeding scalp, having been beaten up by the Gendarmerie for no apparent reason.

And it was these disagreeable people who'd taken over the task of guarding the border between Kivu and Ruanda Burundi, permitting no Congolese to cross over into Ruanda. As UN personnel we were free to come and go, and did so often. In Ruanda's capital Kisenyi, small and far-from-bustling shops still sold useful goods unobtainable in Goma, and on that side of the border we could also buy the delectable telapia.

On Sunday mornings we'd drive to the lakeside where, surrounded by a small crowd of Africans, we'd buy our week-end treat of fish. Noticing on one of these excursions a child not more than six years old carrying his sibling, Roderick remarked with interest,

"Oh look, there's a baby with a baby on his back."

Before Independence overtook the Belgian Congo Kisenyi was a much-favoured place for Belgians, with its beautifully-designed houses surrounded by gardens overlooking Lake Kivu. During our time in Goma, however, most of these houses stood empty – they weren't even occupied by squatters – and few people were visible. One house returning to life belonged to a Belgian woman of Good Family. With its lake-side setting, antiques imported from Europe, and servants both deft and unobtrusive, her home made us realise what an idyllic place for

Europeans this part of Africa had been before Independence in the Belgian Congo put the boot in.

The Malayans made regular sorties into Parc Albert on the Goma side. The purpose of these patrols wasn't clear but it gave them something to do. On one occasion they invited Roderick and me to join them.

Bumping over the rough ground in a Land Rover we stopped at a water-hole to admire and photograph snorting, grunting hippos whose brown faces caught the sun as they broke the surface of the water. A few hundred yards off elephants loomed amongst the trees but they did not approach. We'd been told stories of these animals, who, deciding they didn't like motor vehicles intruding into their territory, had tipped one particular car onto its side. The occupants had then had to sit tight in this awkward position until the herd had ambled off to a safe distance.

CHAPTER 8

Several months into our Goma experience it seemed a good idea to take home leave but then John discovered we hadn't been back in the Congo long enough to have return fares paid by the UN. Nevertheless he agreed that Roderick and I should go for three weeks anyway and he himself would visit Nairobi. Costing far less than a return trip to the UK it held far more appeal for John than a visit to his in-laws.

Back in Africa at the end of our holiday Roderick and I were met at Entebbe airport by John. At the end of the lead he was holding stood a long-legged animal with sticking-out ribs. This was Baski, a Doberman Pinscher who'd been left in Nairobi in the care of a Hindu family until a new, permanent home could be found for him. His previous owners had departed from Kenya for good; they had no desire to stick around and find out how Independence was going to affect white settlers. Friends of this departed couple had persuaded John to take the animal back to Goma. And as the deed was done there was little point in my objecting to this addition to our household.

Baski looked like a famine-victim because the Hindu family had expected him to be a vegetarian like themselves. Apart from denying him meat, however, they had looked after him well and their young son had wept as Baski was led away by his new owner.

The drive from Entebbe to Goma was long and Roderick was sick several times. Possibly he was upset by the smell from the leather-covered seats in the elegant car, a Mercedes lent to John for his Nairobi visit and our collection at Entebbe.

Darkness fell as we drove up to a Ugandan guest house many hours later, thankful to be out of the car at last. After a plain, British-style meal from which Baski was not excluded we all went to bed, Roderick in one corner of the bedroom and the Doberman on a mat between John and me.

In the middle of the night I was woken by a tongue giving my face a quick lick. Baski then lay down again and went back to sleep. This gesture of his disarmed me completely and removed any reservations I had about him; he was so clearly saying "Thank you for taking me on." (Thirty years later a lump still comes to my throat when I think of that kiss).

In a week or two he'd regained his normal elegance, the curve of his hind legs resembling a piece of 18th century furniture. He'd been trained as a puppy by the Nairobi Police and if it hadn't been for the colour prejudice they'd instilled into him his manners could have been described as impeccable. Particularly offensive to Baski for some reason was the sight of a black man riding a bicycle or wearing a hat.

Towards us he was affectionate and obedient. Roderick was especially pleased to have him, remarking with satisfaction as the four of us went on an excursion together for the first time,

"Now we are a family."

The Mercedes belonged to Paul, a Polish doctor. Working with the WHO since June 1960 he had spent most of that time in remote corners of the Congo. He was, John said, respected by the Congolese for his skill and courage. Once, after he'd been robbed during the night, the villagers caught the thief and beat the man almost to death. It took Paul several weeks to restore him to health.

We saw a lot of Paul and upon our first meeting I experienced what the French call a coup de foudre – although I sensed it was infatuation rather than love. (How does one know when powerful attraction is merely infatuation? I have no idea, but it was as strong as it was unexpected). The same height as I, he had dark hair growing into a widow's peak and a smile that weakened my knees. Each time we met my face took on a silly grin I could do nothing to stop.

Paul went away for a few days in order to fetch his wife, just in from

Poland. Also a doctor and as fair as he was dark, Danuta possessed the same calm manner and gentle sense of humour: no question there of a horrid wife who didn't understand her husband. Nevertheless, whenever they dropped in for a meal or for one of the film shows John organised in our living-room, I contrived to sit near Paul. Conversation between us plodded rather than flowed since my French was by no means fluent and his English even less so.

The hospital in Goma was run by another Polish doctor, an enthusiastic communist and very different from Paul: roughly the same height but with curly fair hair and blue eyes from which no warmth shone.

One morning Joseph arrived for work accompanied by his youngest child, a little girl of eight. She had much fever, Joseph told me. He then set to in the kitchen with preparations for our lunch while I drove his daughter to the hospital. Although he could have called in at the hospital with her before coming to work Joseph believed she would have more chance of being attended to if she were accompanied by a 'blanc'.

I'd been warned by people who knew the doctor in charge that he was apt to make everyone, white or black, wait their turn in the yard with all the other patients. Luckily for me he decided to forget the equality bit and Madame was allowed to jump the queue and, although drugs were in short supply, he gave the child a penicillin injection. He then handed me several ampoules of antibiotic to administer over the following few days.

The little girl turned up each morning for her injection, silent and uncomplaining, having walked the two miles from her village. Joseph was pleased with her treatment and swift recovery but plainly considered that my help in the process was the least he expected of his employer.

CHAPTER 9

With Christmas not far off the Colonel decided he'd like a supply of cards. Would I care to accompany the next patrol to Kampala and buy these for him? I accepted the idea with enthusiasm: Kampala was a place where everything still worked and Europeans could buy what they needed.

Roderick was not pleased; apart from the time he'd spent in hospital he and I had never been apart. "I'll bomb the road!" he threatened.

However, mollified by the promise of a present, he allowed me to leave, waving me off as I left with a Malayan sergeant and three corporals for the eight-hour drive. At the Ugandan border our Land Rover was waved through by Congolese soldiers lounging on a bench. They scarcely bothered to look up from their game of cards. On the other side we were greeted by Ugandan police – alert, business-like and welcoming, with boots highly polished and sharp creases in their long, British-colonial-style shorts. The countryside too and villages of round huts topped with conical, thatched roofs looked neat and well cared-for.

In the middle of rough terrain the driver applied his brakes. The men got out and disappeared behind some nearby bushes. Expecting that they would then tactfully make it plain it was my turn to 'go', I stayed where I was, but they climbed back into the vehicle and off we drove. Thanks to everyone's shyness it was in considerable discomfort that I spent the next four hours. Round about tea-time my ordeal came to an end as we arrived at a country hotel on the outskirts of a small town named 'Mbarara. Leaving me to dash to the nearest lavatory the Malayans drove off into town to find themselves overnight accommodation more suited to their purse.

Next morning they collected me for the short drive to Kampala where, with a rendezvous arranged for four o'clock, I was dropped off in the main street.

Having attended to the Colonel's Christmas card order I then had a lovely time buying Christmas presents; also handbag and bathing suit for myself and Noah's Ark for Roderick. Back then for a second night in the hotel that could have been the setting for a Somerset Maugham novel. Men in shorts, shirts and long socks leant against the bar, served by an African immaculate in white jacket, while a ceiling fan turned lazily....

After a good night's sleep in this peaceful place I was collected by my escort for the drive home. This time we stopped at the half-way mark near some large bushes behind whose screen I did what was necessary, the men having sloped off in the other direction.

For those occupying large and secluded houses in Goma, nightwatchmen were essential. An unsmiling Tutsi who towered over us, our man spoke no language we could understand. His clothes consisted of khaki shorts and blanket thrown over one shoulder; a spear with a wicked-looking point completed the outfit. One morning an American friend and I were having coffee when in strode the nightwatchman. He walked up to the young woman and tweaked her breast. Understandably furious she began to berate him. But liking neither his strange smell nor the redness of his eyes I persuaded her to behave as though nothing had happened. He'd clearly been smoking or drinking something powerful. Great was my relief therefore when he turned round and stalked off as silently as he'd come.

Just as we thought our lake-side existence might be going to last for a nice long time, John received word from the UN in Leopoldville to the effect that he must report for another assignment in a matter of weeks. This was a blow. Not only would I have to say goodbye to the cause of my silly grins but I'd be missing an adventure: I'd been invited to join a party of Belgian women on an expedition to gorilla territory in the Mountains of the Moon. It was exasperating to be compelled to miss such an opportunity.

John was also disappointed by the peremptory summons but at least Roderick didn't seem to mind the thought of leaving; he was perhaps glad to get away from the menace of the volcano. (He told us many years later that its glowing summit worried him).

Making the best of things John decided we must throw a party on our last night in Goma.

The fifty guests included Italians, Belgians, French, one Swede, one German, an Irish family, an English coffee-taster and of course our Polish friends. Joseph pulled out all stops over the buffet, while local beer, wine and PX whisky kept things lively.

Lights from every room in the house shone over the garden while music from our record-player must have been heard on the other side of Lake Kivu. I danced with several of our guests and once or twice with John but for each one of these sorties onto the floor I seized two with Paul. We said little as we danced cheek-to-cheek but I longed to drag him outside and behave wantonly on the grass. Glancing over to where Elias seemed to be observing us as he leant against the kitchen door, I knew that such an act wouldn't do. The prospect of not seeing Paul again was painful, though, and never again would I condemn anyone who went off the rails because of an overwhelming passion.

At half-past-two John announced 'Il faut fermer la boutique' – sad words, but necessary if we were to get any sleep before leaving for the airport at 5 a.m. As I prepared for bed I discovered an ear-ring – from the cheek-to-cheek side – was missing. Elias found it while sweeping the floor when the party was over, handing it to me as we left a few hours later. (For months I treasured the ear-ring and the reason for its broken state).

Shortly after five John, Roderick, Baski and I arrived at the airport to find several of our friends already there to see us off. Paul and Danuta were not there.

Waiting to board the plane I found myself standing near the Swedish tea-planter. Something prompted this tall and austere-looking man to remark that the black people busy loading the plane had surely been cast in the role of manual workers by God Himself. He supported his archaic view with a quotation from the Old Testament concerning the sons of Ham. My suggesting it was more important to follow the teachings of the New Testament irritated him: "You know nothing about the real Africa."

More than a little weary I was thankful when we were asked to board the DC4. Meaningful discussions after barely two hours' sleep were not for me.

John ascended the ladder first, leaning down to grasp Baski who was heaved up and into the interior. Lashed together behind the pilots' cabin and giving off a strong but not unpleasant smell lay a mound of fresh vegetables destined for UN personnel in Leopoldville. Baski lay quietly on a piece of sacking next to our seats.

Once airborne we began to feel very cold: we were thankful for our suitcase of blankets, passing one to a white-haired Swiss woman whose grandson huddled against her for warmth. These two were returning to Leopoldville from a holiday in Goma. Roderick and nine-year-old Pierre were soon to become neighbours.

Planning to come to Leopoldville later was Elias who'd asked if he could continue to work for us there while his wife and son stayed behind in Goma. Whether or not Mrs Elias liked this idea she'd evidently have to lump it. She would certainly be thankful for the money that Elias with his faithful nature would undoubtedly be sending her once established in his job in the capital. For us it was comforting to know that this calm and kindly African in his khaki shorts, shirt and old tennis shoes would soon be looking after our household once more.

CHAPTER 10

Houses and flats in Leopoldville were not easy to find. It wasn't only expatriate personnel who were looking for a place to live but returning Belgian families as well. To begin with we occupied the top half of a block-like house built on a rough bit of ground on the outskirts of Parc Hembise, a suburb of executive-type dwellings with enclosed gardens. Next we graduated to a flat over the local bakery in this same suburb, but the heat from the ovens seeping up through the floor forced us to move once more, this time to a pleasant villa with garden on the main road leading into the city.

On the way to work each day John dropped Roderick off at his school, a large establishment run by the Frères Maristes. Amongst the several hundred Congolese boys was a sprinkling of whites.

Since classes began at eight and finished at one, Roderick took with him a sandwich to eat during break but it was usually snatched from him by one of the older boys, many of whom had walked several kilometres to get to school. They weren't only hungry; they tended to fall asleep during lessons. Roderick learnt to do without elevenses .

At least in the afternoons he had Pierre's company. Every Tuesday silence descended on the verandah of our villa as they sat together reading Tintin and Spirou. These magazines were bought by John at the UN bookshop.

With Roderick despatched to his lessons Baski and I would set off for a walk through the lanes, past the silent houses with their high fences and concealing shrubbery. On the first of these walks I made the mistake of letting him off the lead. Almost at once a creature I felt had to be a mastiff appeared in front of us, hackles raised, teeth bared. Too late to grab Baski's collar: with horrible snarls and bared fangs the dogs hurled themselves at each other. Many times did I have to thump the enemy's head with my stick before he broke away and fled.

Blood was everywhere. Our beautiful animal shook his torn ear as though trying to get rid of the pain, splashing me as well as himself. Leading him back to the villa, I phoned John. He came home immediately and together we drove to the vet. To my horror the man took a pair of scissors and snipped off the strip of ear hanging like a piece of ribbon. He then bandaged the ear tightly to the dog's head. On the way home in the car I had to loosen the crepe bandage when I realised Baski was being strangled.

Although after this he stayed on the lead whenever we were out, it didn't put an end to fights. Every male dog we met on the road felt obliged to go for Baski. No doubt the fact that he hadn't been neutered had something to do with it, but whatever the reason the sight of this dark, slinky animal enraged them.

One of our favourite walks took us past the entrance of a mansion, well protected by brick wall and wrought-iron gates. Behind these gates stalked a Great Dane whom Baski delighted in provoking whenever we passed. One day, however, I saw that the gate wasn't shut and the dog was standing outside.

Praying that Baski hadn't noticed – we were still yards away – I pulled him round but, as in all good nightmares, Baski had spotted the other dog. Barking what were no doubt rude and provocative remarks, he gave the Great Dane no option but to attack. I disliked doing it but I thumped the animal on the head with my stick. I knew Great Danes were by nature gentle creatures and I could have wept at the reproachful look he gave me before running off. I could also have kicked Baski for provoking this attack.

The streets of Leopoldville were quiet at that time although break-ins and burglaries happened every day. "Keep some cash in the house" we were told; thieves could turn nasty if they found no money to steal.

In our road most houses sprouted grills over doors and windows and a neighbour of ours kept his VW Beetle chained to a tree at night. Another constructed a pair of low, parallel walls into which his car fitted so snugly it was impossible for anyone to remove wheels, tyres and hubcaps.

One night my sleep was interrupted by a cracking, splitting noise. I got out of bed, trying to judge where the sound had come from, the springs of my bed creaking as they always did. Emerging into the corridor I saw the back door was wide open, a shockingly wrong sight. I dashed back to the bedroom.

"Someone has broken in!"

John leapt out of bed like an erupting volcano, ran into the kitchen and snatched up the rolling-pin but found no-one. We saw, however, where the intruder had squeezed his way into the kitchen: he'd torn away screening along the top of the kitchen window and had wriggled through the resultant ten-inch gap.

As we returned to bed we marvelled at the stroke of luck which had led one of us to forget to double-lock the back door. If we'd done a proper job before going to bed that evening the thief wouldn't have been able to make a rapid escape and I might have come face to face with the sharp end of his machete.

Throughout the excitement Roderick and our watch-dog slept soundly.

The empty shops of Leo took me back to war-time Britain (where finding a box of matches used to represent a small victory) but we could at least buy fruit and vegetables of limited variety in the open market. Spinach, leeks, tomatoes and lettuce appeared frequently at the table. And as UN personnel we could augment our diet with tinned food from the Commissary inside the Royal.

We could also spend Congolese francs at the PX on all kinds of expensive equipment. But satisfying though it was to possess a Zeiss camera, portable typewriter, tape recorder, binoculars and a Canon Zoom, this flaunting of what the haves were enjoying compared with the have-nots took some of the pleasure away. (No wonder also there was so much determined thieving in Leo).

CHAPTER 11

With break-ins in mind John arranged for two Canadian Military Police to sleep overnight in our villa while he himself was away for three days in another province. (Elias had yet to join us from Goma).

As darkness was closing in on the first evening, a jeep drove up and out jumped a young officer accompanied by an older man. The latter told me they'd decided there was little point in their both staying and, avoiding my eye, he drove off. Not pleased with the way in which John's request had been partially ignored, I showed the tall, dark French Canadian where he was to sleep. I then invited him to join me for a beer on the verandah before supper. Roderick was already asleep.

Two hours later we were still sitting on the verandah, my companion having talked non-stop, giving me, victim of my own politeness, no opportunity to break in and suggest we eat.

The subject of prostitution fascinated the young man and having been a police officer in Montreal before his secondment to the Congo he had plenty of anecdotes to relate. At last two or three bottles of beer later he stopped long enough for me to bid him goodnight and escape supperless to bed, my appetite gone. Soon afterwards I heard him clump off to his own room.

When he arrived the following evening my heart sank when I saw a bottle of rye whisky in his hand. Since it was too early to go to bed, however, I sat for a while with my glass of beer and he with his whisky. Once again he launched into a monologue, his evident obsession with sleaze and violence giving me the creeps. At a relatively early hour, therefore, I stood up, bade him goodnight and left him sitting with the bottle beside him.

Once inside the room Roderick and I were sharing during John's absence, I locked the door and made sure the louvred shutters over the windows were securely fastened.

A loud thumping noise shattered my sleep: our so-called protector was trying to get into the bedroom. He then began striking the door with what sounded as though it must have been the butt of his revolver. Roderick slept on in spite of the racket but I sat up in bed, rigid with fear. Any minute this madman was going to start firing at the lock... but then silence. He must have been too drunk to shoot anything or anyone. I heard him weaving off to his room and a bang as he slammed the door.

When I got up the following morning he had already left for the Royal, but there was still a third night to get through. I must ring up his depot and head him off. Then – oh relief! – up drove John, back from his visit a day early.

Shocked by what I told him and angered by the fact his request for two men to look after Roderick and me had been ignored, John lost no time expressing his feelings to the older of the two MPs. The man must have had some inkling of the sort of person his colleague was but had nevertheless let himself be persuaded by the argument that two was company.

One of Roderick's Belgian teachers informed John that his son was behind in Mathematics and therefore needed extra tuition. Only seven he may have been but it was never too early to start laying foundations for success in the Baccalaureat, a qualification spoken of with awe and respect.

Roderick hated these twice-weekly coaching sessions and eventually I told Madame once a week would have to do. He was able to cope with that. When we returned to England the following year Roderick impressed his Primary School teachers with his precocious ability to do complicated metric sums.

There were enjoyable times for Roderick too, with Pierre living nearby, and picnics with other expatriate families could be fun although one of these ended on a sombre note. We'd found a grassy spot alongside the Congo River where we'd eaten our sandwiches in the shade of some trees. As we were packing up to leave we saw a procession appear from round a bend in the track. Followed by a small and silent crowd, four young men carried a litter on which lay a sick young woman. The hostile glances directed at us by these people made me uncomfortable. Our presence was offensive to them and I sensed it was no ordinary GP they were on their way to consult. Fortunately, we all had the wit to maintain a respectful silence while the party disappeared up the track.

On another occasion several families drove to a different section of the river. Here there were sun-warmed rocks to sit on and sparkling water to swim in. After lunch John's boss and I went for a walk in our bathing suits through the waist-high water.

"You know, Mary, there are water-snakes in this river."

"Oh, really?" If he wasn't bothered, why should I be.

Escape from the down-beat atmosphere of Leo could be had by taking a ferry across the river to Congo-Brazzaville. A cheerful place still under French rule, Brazzaville offered excellent meals in open-air restaurants in the tree-lined streets; being able to buy goods long since missing on the other side of the river was also stimulating. On our return from these outings we were charged no duty by the Congolese customs officials as long as our purchases included no French wine or tobacco.

The cool season was dry and sunless. One grey afternoon while Roderick was busy with his Brio train set I decided to make a cake; I had the freedom of the kitchen until Elias returned from his afternoon off.

A metal cupboard held the pots and pans. I reached inside for the cake tins and straightening up became aware of something, an insect probably, on my left shoulder. I gave it a flick. There on the floor was a King Kong of spiders. Even moderately-sized spiders give me the creeps and to think that this thing had been on my shoulder caused me to moan in horror.

Flesh crawling, I backed out of the kitchen and shut the door.

Roderick mustn't see this monster. He didn't like spiders either.

Needing some sort of physical contact, I hugged Baski who was enjoying his after-lunch siesta on the sitting-room sofa. He grunted affectionately as I clung to him for a minute or two before returning to the kitchen.

The next step was to despatch the creature. It could well have been harmless and perhaps even of a rare species but it had to go.

With a thick Larousse dictionary wrapped in newspaper I opened the door and there was the spider, huge and horrible in the middle of the floor. Holding the dictionary up high and shutting my eyes I dropped the heavy book and fled.

On his return I told Elias about the 'grande araignée morte' in the kitchen. Spiders shrivel and usually look much smaller when they are dead but this one's corpse was impressive enough to startle Elias when he'd removed the dictionary.

"Wapi! " he exclaimed.

CHAPTER 12

Several weeks before Christmas John came home with exciting news: the manager of the PX – where UN personnel could buy such essentials as Vat 69 whisky, American cigarettes and cosmetics – had organised a shipment of toys from the United States.

On the appointed day a long queue of UN employees formed outside the PX, my Greek friend Mary and I being at the front. We'd arrived at least an hour early. The doors opened and the first batch of twenty parents were admitted, each of us being entitled to buy up to four presents for each child. Some people appeared to be shopping for a dozen offspring at least.

The bargeing and grabbing created an unlovely atmosphere cheapened further by a saccharine rendering of 'I'm dreaming of a white Christmas' oozing out of the loud-speaker. Conscious of the fact that I hadn't spared a thought for anyone else's child I slunk out of the building with my parcels. I was thankful to climb into the car and drive away from the silent crowd of Congolese spectators.

Roderick's pleasure on Christmas morning more than compensated for any feelings of guilt.

'Merci pour le joli avion!' he exclaimed upon finding amongst the parcels at the foot of his bed a large friction toy Boeing.

After breakfast he announced:

"Aujourd'hui on va à la Messe," repeating what he'd been told at school.

We didn't go to Mass but to a carol service in the Baptist Church where, dressed in Sunday best, American families predominated.

1964 brought with it rumours of rebel forces heading for Leopoldville. For this reason I didn't fly home to see my gentle father before he died from cancer: I was afraid I might not get back. If things turned ugly in Leo I did not want to be separated from Roderick. (In the month of May after barely a week in hospital Daddy died).

A Scottish friend of ours was given the task of organising the evacuation of UN families to the comparative safety of the Royal in the event of an attack. And it was during this period of tension that the Admin Officer did a John Wayne act, except it wasn't settlers being rescued from the redskins but a party of Unesco teachers and their families from Congolese rebels.

The teachers had fled with their belongings to the shore of Lake Tanganyika at Usumbura, there to await rescue. Surrounding them were hordes of Congolese jumping up and down in ragged remnants of uniform, spears and other home-made weapons much in evidence. The fact that they all appeared to be drunk made the scene that much more terrifying for the Europeans.

Accompanied by a young Frenchman John had to travel across the lake by steamer and bring the refugees to safety. When he and his colleague disembarked they found the families huddled together on the beach. John wondered how on earth he was to convey amiable intentions to the banana-wine-influenced warriors hopping up and down in the background. Fortunately, he knew that if in Belgian fashion he attempted to shake hands with any of these people such contamination by a European could mean he'd be slain on the spot. Thankful therefore that the absence of hair on the top of his head meant he always wore a hat, John was able to demonstrate goodwill by raising his trilby in a courtly manner.

Whether it was this gesture on the part of the UN official or whether the need to find more banana wine suddenly became paramount John couldn't tell. But no attempt was made to prevent him and his assistant from herding the nervous families up into the safety of the steamer.

Many needed an exasperating amount of persuasion to leave their possessions behind; space on board was limited and John knew the temper of the rebels could explode at any minute. He and his colleague had difficulty in keeping their cool with people unable to comprehend the need to get away fast. Finally, the gangplank was raised and an ever-widening gap was put between the rescued and the menace on the beach.

Months later John and the other young man received telegrams of congratulations for their rescue act from the UN Secretary-General Ralph Bunche.

For two reasons, apart from the obvious one, the rumours of a rebel advance in our direction filled me with unease. Roderick was soon to become a new boy at the College Albert in Leo, a school run on French lines and highly regarded by the Belgians. John the Francophile was pleased to think his son was to become one of its pupils. There was every chance, however, that no sooner had Roderick started there than we'd have to pull out of the Congo. And in his seven years of life Roderick had already been to seven different schools .

If, as he hoped, John continued to work for the UN we were inevitably going to be on the move, often after a matter of months. I began to reflect that boarding school, something I'd declared as a teenager I'd never inflict on my children, might be a better fate for Roderick than the constant changes he did not enjoy.

A second factor influencing my thoughts was the knowledge that I was probably pregnant. I'd given up all hope of this ever happening again and in spite of obvious indications I couldn't believe my good fortune.

The suspense of not knowing for certain was unbearable. I went to see the doctor to ask if he could confirm whether I was or wasn't pregnant.

"Get your boy to catch a frog, bring it here, and we'll do a test."

I asked Elias~to find a 'grenouille'. Puzzled by this request but too well mannered to comment, he brought me a jam jar half full of frogs the size of a thumb nail. I guessed that such miniscule creatures were not what the doctor had in mind but not wishing to hurt Elias's feelings I waited until he'd returned to the kitchen before tipping the contents of the jar into a flower bed.

After several days of being sickened whenever the smell of John's cigars wafted my way I dared hope there was no need for a frog to confirm that I was pregnant.

I knew the staff of the WHO hospital in Leo were perfectly capable of delivering and caring for babies, but would they cope with mine who because of my Rh Negative blood group might need a total transfusion soon after birth? I wanted the precious infant to be born in England. This desire, coupled with the wish to avoid for Roderick a sudden yanking out of school because of rebels, enabled me to insist that the two of us return to Britain. By this time we even had a home of our own to go to.

The year before we'd bought a 17th century cottage in Norfolk thirteen miles from my brother's house. £1,700 it cost, most of the money being borrowed from the Bank. No more would we have to dump ourselves on long-suffering family every time leave came up.

Once again John was left behind to complete the last few months of his contract when Roderick and I took the Sabena Airlines flight home to England. Baski flew separately to London airport where he was collected and taken to kennels for a long spell in quarantine.

With the August sunshine slanting into our south-facing cottage Roderick and I arrived in Briningham. He was happy to be home and to discover the delights of English television, especially the pleasurably terrifying Darleks. The prospect of boarding school thrilled him less. First, though, he was to spend a year at day school.

"I like this easy school!" was how he greeted me as he emerged from his first day at Holt Primary.

Meanwhile in Leopoldville the threat of advancing rebels had melted away. As his contract drew to an end John succeeded in getting his foot in the door of another UN agency. Delighted to be leaving the Congo he flew off in the New Year to report for duty with the Food and Agriculture Organisation in Rome.

PART VI

ROME
1965

CHAPTER 1

Established in a three-bedroomed flat borrowed from people on leave, John discovered the existence of St George's English School. He therefore telephoned to say he'd be over by car in a few weeks time to take Roderick back with him. He was missing his son and felt that life in a small village with a pregnant mother couldn't be fun for an eight-year-old. In due course Dad arrived and after a brief stay in Briningham he left with Roderick for the long drive down to Rome.

Miranda's arrival on the 3rd April was so swift she narrowly missed being born in my brother Desmond's MG. I'd been staying for the previous few days with my mother and brother in Wells-next-the-sea. When late in the evening I announced that labour had started, cross words were exchanged between them since one or the other had failed to collect the family car from its service that afternoon.

The bucket seat of the sports car was tremendously comfortable, however, and Desmond kept my mind off the accelerating contractions by suggesting babies' names – most of them hilariously awful – as we sped along the coast road to the maternity home twenty miles away. An hour after he'd left me with the Night Sister the baby was born.

A week later my sister Margaret arrived from Warwickshire with her two small children to stay with us for Miranda's first week in Rose Cottage. One of the practical things she did was to take me to buy a spin-drier for the nappies. They'd have taken ages to dry in the showery April weather and the house wasn't warm. The only heating we had was an open fire in the sitting-room and paraffin stoves in the bedrooms. But my sister and her children were used to such conditions. Their house, a former bakery, had its cool zones too.

When she had reached the age of five weeks Miranda and I set off from London to join the rest of the family in Rome. The passengers on board the Air Alitalia flight quickly taught me several Italian words and phrases; for example: "Quanti mesi?", "Carina!" and "Bellissima!" And although I knew that to dote on all babies and children came naturally to Italians, their admiration for Miranda went down well.

Meeting us at the airport Roderick was pleased with his sister although disappointed I hadn't taken his advice to call her Mary-Ann. John had chosen the name Charlotte and for the first hour or two of her life this was what was written on the label over her cot in the maternity home. When later I'd had a second look at this baby with rosy cheeks and hair the colour of dark gold I felt the name was not going to suit her. Charlotte was crossed out and Miranda inserted instead.

The American family who had lent John their flat owned an Alsatian dog. For many evenings after we moved in John and I sat with our gin and tonics, leaning over every now and then to pick up and drown in a glass of water one of the many fleas hopping about in the carpet.

"How revolting!" I shuddered.

(Years later I took back these disapproving words when our own house suffered from displaced fleas following the death of our cat).

The suburb we were living in formed part of Rome known as EUR – Expositione Universale di Roma – built in Mussolini's heyday. Outside the metro stop for EUR immense statues of horses reared up, towering above heroic figures of men guarding the entrance to the permanent exhibition. Except for these reminders of Il Duce's passion for grandiose structures, EUR resembled any city suburb with its flats, large supermarket, an elegant shop selling beautifully-made and beautifully-smelling leather bags, belts and cases, and another shop outside which I often lingered but never entered, offering babies' and children's garments, exquisite and impossibly expensive.

Every morning after breakfast Roderick set off in his maroon cap and blazer for the short walk to St George's, turning frequently to wave to Mickey Mouse who stood on the balcony waving back.

One Saturday afternoon Roderick and an American boy of the same age came panting into the flat. With fear in his voice Roderick told us they'd inadvertently set a workman's shelter alight on the pavement down below. They feared that for the second time Rome was about to burn. John dashed down to investigate the disaster and found that the small camp fire the boys had made from rubbish had flared up and burnt part of the canvas shelter. By the time he got there, the conflagration had fizzled out.

We did our best to reassure the children that they had caused no serious damage but this attitude was not shared by Roderick's friend's mother. When her son told her what had happened she came bursting into our flat with him in tow.

"This is Vandalism!" she informed us.

And to her son: "You wait until your Dad gets home!"

In vain did we try to convince her it had obviously been an accident and nothing too dreadful had happened. Off she stormed dragging her frightened son after her, while John and I pondered uneasily over the probable fate of the unfortunate small boy.

We shared the services of Emilia our maid with an Italian family living nearby. Her 8 to 12 employer worked her hard, she told us, and she sighed frequently that she was tired. I had noticed that on most week-day mornings a thudding noise came from flat balconies onto which carpets had been heaved for a daily beating. Lugging these heavy objects about must have been exhausting for the maids.

Emilia liked the baby and was happy to be left in charge of her while I drove Roderick and friends to the beach, our favourite after-school goal.

The sea was warm and the sand the colour of pumice stone. On Sundays whole families set up camp with awnings, umbrellas, tables, chairs and portable stoves on which to cook the pasta. We took Miranda with us once but even shaded by an umbrella it was too hot for her.

One Sunday we went for a picnic along the Appian Way, marvelling at the still-useful paving stones dating back to ancient times. We sat in the shade of small trees expecting any moment to hear the thudding and clanking of Legions approaching.... At the same time we kept a look-out for vipers we'd been warned might appear in the grass.

In the pale blue pram John had bought in the market Miranda accompanied us on a visit to Hadrian's Villa, a satisfying ruin with its large formal pool edged by statues, some without heads. But this expedition didn't suit her since the ground was rough and her pram not particularly well sprung. She cried much that evening.

Several friends came to stay, including my school friend Mary who did Rome thoroughly. Descending the Spanish Steps she was importuned by a young man who refused to be shaken off, finally melting away when she made it plain she really was more interested in antiquities than in his handsome person.

Paul came back into my life briefly when he and Danuta visited over a long week-end. ("Quel enfant sage!" he said of Miranda who hardly ever cried). We went swimming, and while the others waded back onto the beach to dry themselves and stretch out in the sun, Paul and I stayed in the deep water, holding hands as the waves gently rocked us. Although I still felt great warmth for him, the fire had gone out. Just as well, of course.

The 1960s Romans we encountered weren't noticeably friendly, one exception being a teenage boy who worked in the supermarket. When Miranda's blue pram arrived inside the doors he'd stop whatever he was doing to hover beside it and keep her company while I shopped.

To be smartly dressed was important in that city and I rated poorly, wearing as I did home-made cotton dresses and flat-heeled sandals. The inexpensive pram didn't help my image either.

CHAPTER 2

As the heat of the summer climbed towards its peak we kept away from the scorching beach. A Belgian family we'd met in the Congo invited Roderick to spend two weeks with them at the Belgian seaside. Roderick seemed to like the idea and we accepted on his behalf. As the Boeing started to taxi down the runway a hand waved to us from the window. Tears fell down my cheeks as the aircraft roared vertically into the sky and on its way to Brussels.

John then decided we should take this opportunity to have a three-day holiday on our own. Emilia welcomed the chance of earning extra by looking after Miranda in her neat house at Ostia, but I was far from happy about leaving our baby behind. I feared she'd be kidnapped because soon after my arrival in Rome John had told me how difficult it was for childless couples in Italy to find babies since the adoption rules were impossibly strict. To me it seemed entirely logical therefore that while we were away Emilia would be tempted to make herself a small fortune by selling this exquisite baby to some couple with funds to match their desperation for a child.

In spite of these misgivings I handed Miranda over to Emilia and off we drove to a small hotel in Paestum, a place of blue sea, solitary beaches and lovely ruins warm to the touch in the July sun.

The first evening I could hardly wait to phone Emilia to ask if all was well. I was momentarily reassured by her assurances of "multo dormire" and "multo mangare". So great was my neurotic anxiety, however, that as soon as we'd finished our rudimentary conversation I began to wonder, "Was that really Emilia or was it someone pretending to be her while she herself was miles away handing over our baby for a fistful of lira?" Naturally John didn't share these dreads and of course when we returned to Rome two days later we found Miranda at Emilia's with a wet nappy but beaming at us from her cot when we walked in through the door.

On the 1st September we woke to find that summer had come to an end.

Yesterday's blue skies had became grey and hitherto undetected draughts in the flat sought out our ankles. We didn't mind too much therefore when John's boss told him he was shortly to be sent to an FAO project in Teheran. Roderick, the baby and I would return to Briningham.

John's idea was that Miranda and I should join him in Teheran as soon as the autumn term started up, whereas I wanted to help Roderick ease into his new boarding school experience by staying at our cottage for the duration of his first term. Then I'd be able to visit and he could come home for week-ends. John wasn't pleased but had to put up with it.

Once home my first task was to fetch Baski from quarantine kennels where, because of the timing of our comings and goings, he had had to spend a year. We'd been sent monthly bulletins on our dog's state of health by the kennels owner – "Baski is in good spirits" and "Baski is eating well" were his usual comments. It was therefore no surprise to see the top half of a healthy-looking Baski leaning on the half-door of his kennel, barking at his neighbours. He greeted the kennels owner with affection but when brought over to us merely jumped into the back of the car and sat down. Once we reached Rose Cottage, however, he bounded out and went berserk, tearing round the garden like a rocket. Finally skidding to a halt, he hurled himself at me, grinning and grinning. Recognition and the realisation of freedom had struck.

In spite of the long spell in quarantine his spirit appeared undamaged although wherever I went – upstairs, downstairs, into the garden – he stuck to my heels, causing Roderick to nickname him Glue. (When the time came to take Roderick to his boarding school for the first time and later after weekend visits home, Baski and his imaginary exploits provided a diversion, alleviating the gloom of these occasions).

At the end of the Christmas term the boys at Beeston Hall wrote and produced a Nativity play. Clothed in a dress with bath-towel headdress, Roderick as Mary is found sweeping the floor by the Angel Gabriel.

"Why has God chosen me to have His baby?"

"Because he thinks you would make a good mother."

On this sensible note the term ended and Roderick came home to Rose Cottage.

Part VII

TEHERAN
1967

CHAPTER 1

The holidays for Roderick came and went, he, Miranda and I having spent Christmas with my mother in Wells. On Boxing Day John had telephoned from Teheran. He wanted Miranda and me to join him once school restarted. Originally he'd decided if we couldn't join him there from the beginning we might as well sit it out in Briningham, since his stay in Iran was to be a limited one, but he'd changed his mind.

Having looked forward to a longish stay at Rose Cottage and being within easy reach of Roderick's school for a few more months, I wasn't entirely pleased. However, from what John said Iran was fascinating and Teheran not the sort of place we'd normally expect to visit. Roderick would of course join us for the Easter holidays.

But Baski'd have to stay behind. Even had there been no quarantine laws in Britain, Teheran wouldn't have been the place for a dog, especially such a large one. He had by this time spent the occasional night or two in a Sheringham kennels whose owner treated him as one of the family. Therefore I didn't feel too badly about leaving him. It couldn't be helped, anyway.

With the help of my friend Doris from the other end of the village I tidied the house, locking away small treasures and breakable objects into the cupboard under the stairs. During our absence the cottage was to be let to summer visitors and bird watchers.

Half way through January, Miranda and I set off in a hired car for London Airport where we caught the flight for Teheran.

John was there to greet us as we arrived in the middle of the night. He tactlessly remarked that Miranda, sitting up in her carry-cot and taking everything in, looked like a rugger player. This observation was no doubt prompted by the fact that her nose hadn't lost the flattening it had received at birth. (Offended on her behalf though I was, I had to admit her nose had bothered me at first until the midwife assured me the strange shape would be a temporary phenomenon).

Waiting for the luggage to be unloaded I felt chilled by the silence of the unsmiling porters in their blue overalls. An unsocial hour it undoubtedly was but they didn't even appear interested in the prospect of a tip, just as well, since they didn't get one.

Through the silent streets of Teheran we drove until our headlights picked out a doorway set into a high wall. John stopped the car and we all got out. Unlocking the door he led us through into a small garden shaded by trees. An outside light glimmered on the surface of a pool divided into two by a raised path. And overlooking garden and pool stood a three-storeyed building, each level fronted by a balcony the size of a small room. Woven blinds were rolled up in readiness for the heat of sumner when the glare of the sun would have to be kept at bay.

In January, however, it was cold and next morning, standing on the balcony of our second-floor flat, John pointed out distant mountains covered in snow.

As the months progressed the snow blanket would creep up the mountainside until reaching the summit it disappeared altogether. Summer heat had by then taken over and very pleased we were to find the deep, cool water of our ornamental pool.

The streets of Teheran were dull and dusty-looking. Most of the women wore the chador, a length of thin material enveloping their bodies from head to ankle. This garment had no fastenings but as she walked along a woman could be seen gripping the top edges of the material between her teeth, leaving hands free for handbag and shopping basket. In winter-time the chador was black, to be replaced in the spring by a greyish-white version. With the advent of these light-coloured chadors – garments that did nothing to brighten the scene – men in black suits and collarless shirts could be observed drinking tea in side-walk cafes.

Venturing into town by car could be hazardous. The numerous taxi drivers earned little and competition amongst them was fierce. Without warning a taxi would swoop across the street to the kerb if the driver considered there existed the smallest chance of picking up a fare. They saw no reason either to limit the number of people they stopped for.

One afternoon I was sitting in a taxi on my way to work when the vehicle came to a halt to allow two men to get in, one in the front and one next to me at the back. They evidently knew the driver well and as we drove along I answered their questions as well as I could in my limited Farsi. Their nosiness about where I was going and what I was doing in Teheran was good-natured rather than offensive.

The covered market afforded many temptations. Throughout its network of little streets stood small shops and stalls displaying locally-made goods and artefacts. For a modest price you could buy that essential 1960s garment, a long sheepskin jacket – irresistible until you came close enough to breath in its animal smell. Some stage in the process of turning raw skin into garment had been missed out. What I coveted most, however, was a brooch or pair of earrings made from silver and turquoise but they were too expensive, as were the rugs and carpets. Shop after shop stocked these beauties, many of them spread over the pavement for people to walk on. When the carpet was new this improved the pile.

Shopping for groceries presented no problem. IranSuper's shelves were stocked with the sort of things we were used to and as in all supermarkets the goods were labelled and priced; the ability to speak Farsi was not required of its customers. Also stocked were locally-made household articles and toys: the miniature red enamel cooking pot with lid I found in IranSuper became one of Miranda's favourite possessions.

Not tempted to patronise the cubby-holes where meat hung from hooks in unrecognisable hanks I bought the Sunday joint from a European-style butcher; the purchase of fruit and vegetables from the market became the responsibility of our maid.

Suhani arrived for work each day wearing the chador and looking a little like a witch with her black hair, pale face and bad teeth, but she was good-natured and worked hard. Underneath her chador she wore western clothes, white winkle-picker shoes being exchanged for slippers once she was inside the flat. Since she spoke no English we had to communicate in Farsi with the help of grammar-book and dictionary.

An Iranian couple lived in the middle flat. Members of the Zoroastrian faith they were gentle people but sad. This was because of the failure of a longed-for baby to materialise and the background of unease against which they lived. They spoke nervously of the secret police who lurked everywhere.

The young woman became fond of Miranda and liked to take her for a swim in the garden pool. Always happy to baby-sit, she'd refuse to accept payment but as she'd admired a pair of knee-high boots of mine, I gave her this other important part of a woman's 1960s wardrobe and she was pleased; boots of this kind couldn't be found in Teheran and my friend was as fashion-conscious as the next Iranian woman.

Through his work in the FAO John got to know several Iranians as well as the expatriates: British, American, French and German. These people were all providing technical assistance on behalf of UN agencies. During an evening reception for this mixed bag of nationalities John introduced me to the wife of an Iranian government minister. This Iranian woman Zara was a well-educated, warm-hearted person. Even she couldn't entirely relax, however, and during our times together when often there might be no one in the room apart from herself, John and me, she always spoke of the Shah as "His Imperial Majesty". Perhaps it was natural to her to refer to him in this formal manner but I had the impression that were she to speak of him simply as "the Shah" she could have been in trouble.

CHAPTER 2

Iranians loved to entertain, especially on a grand scale, and soon after my arrival John and I were invited to a fancy-dress ball. The costumes were lavish. I hadn't expected such sophistication and elegance but discovered that although little choice in ready-made clothes was to be found in the shops there were women whose skills made up for this lack.

John took me to meet a dressmaker recommended to him by the wife of a colleague. From eastern Europe this hard-working person had an Iranian husband.

Anna employed several women to do the cutting and pinning and she could produce a dress in any style you chose. Show her an illustration in Vogue and she'd copy it. She was far from happy, however. She longed to get away from Teheran and the husband who treated her as his property; his view was that she should consider herself fortunate to be his wife. He also made certain she stayed put by refusing to let her have a passport of her own. Without his permission she had no hope of getting one. She was well and truly stuck.

During one of my visits Anna told me about the religious processions that at certain times of the year could be seen winding through the streets. In the old days to show their penitence men would beat themselves with swords and chains as they marched until the blood ran. But the Shah had outlawed this public display of self-punishment.

From the balcony of our flat I watched one of these processions.

Although no one was beating himself the atmosphere of gloom pervading the scene drove me back inside, into the cheerful presence of our cuddly baby daughter.

A winter diversion for those who could afford it was to ski on the nearby mountains while beyond the city in another direction lay the polo club. This I was pleased to discover had none of the snooty atmosphere prevailing in its Lagos counterpart. The Elburz mountains with their white covering diminishing as spring approached formed a backdrop to the game, while horses and riders in the foreground created a spectacle of interest for Miranda in her push-chair.

On Friday, the day of rest, whole families picnicked on the grass alongside the roads leading out of the city, men in black suits, small boys dressed like their fathers, little girls wearing long stockings under their coats and women in the inevitable chador. Beside each family sat a samovar of tea, the favourite beverage. Zara told me that the most welcome present to give an Iranian was a packet of Darjeeling. We had noticed that whenever we had a pot of tea in the flat Suhani kept any left in the pot to reheat for herself later.

With the warmth of spring still to come John was asked to visit FAO experts working near the Caspian Sea, a trip he decided could be combined with a short holiday for himself and me. We left Miranda with an English couple who'd become for us in Teheran the nearest thing to best friends in this cocktail-party-circuit life we were leading. We set off northwards in a Land Rover accompanied by two Danes also employed by the FAO, an Iranian driver at the wheel.

Craggy brown mountains loomed beside us as we sped along a road much in need of gritting. When the driver's carefree manner of negotiating the slippery surface on the sharp bends had given us all curly toes for long enough John and he changed places.

The route took us through several tunnels cut through the mountains; driving into one of these we were dazzled by the sun at the other end glittering on a cluster of icicles hanging from the roof.

After an hour or two we left the mountains behind and arrived at Barbasol, a small seaside town, bleak in the rain. Grey sea was visible behind the hotel towards which we drove. Formerly one of the Shah's palaces, this hotel boasted high-ceilinged bedrooms with adjoining bathrooms. The baths standing on clawed feet may have been stained but the western-style plumbing was a welcome sight and a relief after the Turkish lavatory we'd used en route.

Descending the broad staircase after a lukewarm bath we found our way to the dining-room where a table had been set for the four of us and the hotel manager. Our meal over, the manager switched on a record player and while John danced with the Danish expert's wife I quick-stepped with the tall and rather good-looking manager, over a carpet the size of a tennis court. The fact that there were only five of us could have made all this space unnerving. However, the vodka our host supplied counteracted any feeling of agrophobia or depression caused by the atmosphere of out-of-season dreariness.

Next morning we continued our journey. Mists covered the fields, softening the outline of distant mountains. The sky was pale blue. Rice fields glistened behind clusters of small, thatched-roofed dwellings perched on stilts. The only form of transport we saw were horses and donkeys; a cart drawn by a horse with a high wooden collar evoked images of Russia.

We overtook a tall figure wearing a hat made of lamb's skin. The front view of his long cloak resembled a brown paper bag cut down the middle. A feeling we might at any moment meet Hereward the Wake striding along was heightened at the sight of a second man wearing shoes of animal skin and cross-garters over his trousers.

Reaching the village where our experts were stationed we were grateful for the lunch of roast lamb they had prepared for us. With business completed some hours later we drove back; this time without an overnight stop, back to Teheran and the 20th century.

John's next out-of-town sortie was to Isfahan, a city rich in Persian art and antiquities. This time he went on his own. On the first day of his four-day absence our English friends took Miranda and me for a drive into the countryside. Once again it was towards the mountains that we headed. In the middle distance were hills seemingly covered with grey-green velvet, while at the side of the road a small stream bounded over the rocks. Miniature poplars stood to attention and small bushes my friends told me were junipers dotted the hillsides. As we drove through a village the car was chased by a cheerful group of brown-skinned boys with cropped heads and cold sores. A small dog with clipped ears ran along at their heels.

At this point Valerie's two-year-old son was sick over her smart black overcoat. It was time to go home. Throughout the drive Miranda had stayed awake, sucking her forefinger while murmuring in contented fashion.

Roderick joined us at the end of March for the Easter holidays. During the drive from the airport in the early hours he gave us a blow-by-blow description of the latest Dr Who episode, but his voice sounded muffled, as though his throat were not quite right. In the light of the street lamps he looked washed out.

After a few hours' sleep he was up and inspecting his sister, now a year old. He pronounced himself pleased with her – a tough little thing in his view – while she lay on the floor in a fit of shyness, at the same time peeping up at him with a smile.

Later that day I took Roderick to a doctor who said his tonsils were in such a bad state they should come out as soon as the infection had responded to antibiotics. Meanwhile, in spite of his tonsils Roderick didn't appear to be feeling ill and after a few days confined to the flat he discovered that Teheran was a pretty good place to be. There were plenty of children of his own age who invited him to their houses and to the cinema.

Ten days after his arrival we took Roderick to the Teheran Clinic on the appointed day for his operation. The Iranian surgeon had explained beforehand that it was his practice after removing tonsils to suture the spot where they'd been, thus making post-operative haemorrhage unlikely. Whether this was a procedure automatically followed by British surgeons I didn't know but I felt confidence in this Iranian with his beautiful small hands and gentle manner.

Sitting with Roderick as he came round from the anaesthetic I was thankful when the nurse looking after him felt able to give an injection for relief of pain. By evening this had become bearable and he was allowed to go home. One week later he resumed his social life, learning to ride and enjoying once more the cinema visits and meals in restaurants with other children.

When the time came to return to school Roderick didn't appear depressed, only insisting that Miranda should see him off at the airport. A Universal Aunt would meet him at the other end and put him on the school train at Liverpool Street. Having out-of-the-ordinary occurrences to describe to his friends was perhaps going to offset the pangs of homesickness.

CHAPTER 3

Soon after Roderick's departure John and I were invited by an American couple to accompany then to an "authentically Persian event". Inside a bell-shaped building lined with mirrors and coloured tiles, tiers of seats encircled a small, octagonal arena surfaced with sand. A group of men of all ages appeared from off-stage, each wearing embroidered knee britches and a red shawl draped over one shoulder. The shawls were placed on a low wall dividing the arena from the audience and to the beat of a drum the performance began. A huge fellow who must have been nearly seven feet tall lay on his back holding in each hand a slab of wood the size of a small door. With immense effort and by locking his big toes together he managed to raise and lower the heavy wooden objects several times. He seemed to be tested to the limit of his strength since in spite of his great size he was pale and not noticeably muscular. His ordeal was uncomfortable to watch.

Chanting as they did so the other athletes then performed exercises, their leader a fat man in a green track-suit. During push-ups legs and feet became entangled in the limited space but no one displayed irritation. Next they swung heavy clubs for a while. Then several of them took turns to spin round and round at incredible speed, causing hands and arms to turn red. Abruptly putting on the brakes and with no wobbling at all they'd then walk back to the wall to mop up the sweat with a red shawl. One old chap spun on his own to the cheers of his colleagues.

Audible above the thudding of the drum was a vocal accompaniment to the performance: verses by a Persian poet named Ferdowsi, declaimed by a man perched high above the scene.

Throughout the proceedings the atmosphere was solemn, and it was touching to observe the affection and consideration shown by the performers towards each other; if there was any spirit of competitiveness amongst them it wasn't discernible.

The English friends who'd taken Miranda and me for the drive into the countryside were soon to leave Teheran for good. When I mentioned to Valerie that I'd like to find a part-time job she put me in touch with the doctor for whom she had been doing secretarial work. Dr X was one of Teheran's leading obstetrician-gynaecologists.

Valerie took me to meet him, and learning that I'd studied nursing in Edinburgh he offered me the post of "English-language secretary and office nurse" five evenings a week. An Iranian girl worked for him during the day. When I pointed out I had completed half my training only, he assured me that even so I would have received more training than most of his nurses.

With dark hair, brown eyes and a stocky build my part-time employer proved to be a great wheeler-dealer. Much of the correspondence I typed for him had nothing to do with medicine but concerned his business interests. These included desalination plants; the proposed export of Caspian Sea prawns and the importation of one-arm bandits. This latter project was making no headway at all, I was glad to hear.

The secretarial part of my work completed and wearing a white cap and overall, I spent the ensuing two hours in the consulting room. Principal duties were to hand the doctor his sterile rubber gloves and to pass him whatever size speculum he asked for. Some of his Muslim patients suffered cruelly from embarrassment, covering their faces with their hands while they were examined.

Dr X told me his patients were pleased a British woman was helping him during his evening surgery. This was not as I smugly surmised because they recognised in me someone who was above gossiping about who'd been in and for what, but because knowing so little Farsi I couldn' t gossip.

I was gratified when Dr X announced one day he was going to teach me all he could about gynaecology. (I felt as excited over this as I had when Mr Cromwell New York had made a similar proposal). The next time therefore a patient was brought into his surgery writhing with the pain of a miscarriage he took me along to the Clinic so I could see what the procedure was.

The suffering woman was laid on the operating table but it was ages before the anaesthetist succeeded in finding a vein into which to inject the drug that would render her unconscious. I was deeply shocked also when, having dropped the swab he was about to use, he picked it up from the floor and wiped the patient's skin with it. Although Dr X made no protest, an act as sloppy as this would have been regarded with horror at the Edinburgh Royal.

On another occasion I watched Dr X deliver a baby – its head resembling a shelled walnut as it emerged but quickly filling out to acquire a human appearance.

Although the woman had obviously been suffering during the latter part of labour my boss assured me she would not remember the pain afterwards since he'd given her "twilight sleep". What sort of compensation was that, I asked him, since her pain had in no way been alleviated; but he wasn't interested in discussing this. He was after all the expert.

Having been thanked profusely by the new mother's family, he took me along to see a patient on whom he had recently operated free of charge. As he stood by her bed she took his hand and kissed it. Dr X couldn't resist glancing at me to see if I'd observed the gesture. He was rather touched by it himself.

With the end of our stay in Teheran approaching Suhani had to give up her job because of ill health. In her place came Ossiah, an individual of sturdy proportions – strong enough to wash carpets, was how Zara put it – with brown hair pulled back into a bun and a smile revealing an impessive number of gold teeth. A good cook, she disapproved of my serving meat during the hot weather. It would heat the blood, she managed to convey, and showed me some of her vegetarian dishes. Neither did she approve of the water-filled contraption John had borrowed and which gurgled away all night cooling the air of our bedroom.

When the time came to break the news to Dr X that John's contract was coming to an end and we'd be leaving Teheran at the end of July he asked me if I couldn't stay on. The fact that I had a husband who would certainly wish me to accompany him to his next post was evidently an unimportant detail. Finding a flat for me and the two children would present no problem, he asssured me, and as for the work permit – no problem either:

"The wife of the Minister of Labour is a patient of mine!"

However, he accepted with good grace my having to go and we parted on terms of mutual esteem.

Before I left, Ossiah and I went round the flat earmarking furniture, carpeting and household goods John and I wouldn't be taking with us and that she could keep after we'd gone. She'd described her small house in a Teheran suburb, telling me it had no coverings on the concrete floors, so that it was satisfying envisaging the improvements her spartan dwelling was about to enjoy. Most of what we were giving her was second- and even third-hand – passed on from one expatriate to another – but this transaction gave us both satisfaction.

With the thermometer reading 110 F and climbing, Miranda and I left for London by air on the 30th July. John would follow a few weeks later. After a night in the Grosvenor Hotel we spent the week-end in Hitchin with Mary, Miranda's godmother. Then it was off to Norfolk to collect Roderick from a school-friend's house in King's Lynn, and Baski from kennels in Sheringham.

Part VIII

SENEGAL
1968

CHAPTER 1

Senegal in former French West Africa was to be the scene of John's next posting. Baski was enjoying his new life as companion to a builder, Roderick putting up with being back at school, while Miranda aged two enjoyed anything that came along.

Living with us once more at Rose Cottage our lovely Doberman had proved to be a magnet for every dog we met. Each one felt obliged to attack him and had to be beaten off with my walking stick. Particularly hostile towards Baski was our next-door neighbour's dog, a sad mongrel who spent his days tied up at the end of a piece of rope inside the gate to his owner's property. Every time Bonzo spotted our Baski he went berserk until one afternoon his rope snapped. A terrible fight ensued during which my legs became entangled with lead and snarling dogs. Bonzo bit me on the calf. It hurt like anything, but apart from two holes in my leg I suffered no serious harm.

The wounds inflicted on each other by the two dogs meant urgent visits to the vet. Later that day my neighbour stormed round to my back door to complain about "that vicious brute" Baski. I never saw Bonzo again. I suspected his evil-tempered owner had had him put to sleep or, to save expense, had shot the dog himself.

Much as I loved Baski our walks were nerve-wracking and when not out for a walk he became bored. He needed to be active and did not need owners constantly going off abroad. I therefore appealed for help to the kennels-owner in Sheringham and he agreed to help find a dog-lover who could give Baski the companionship and stimulation he craved.

The ideal owner was found – a builder wanting a dog to take with him on his drives round the sites. With him Baski had found his niche. When not lording it over the builder's family in their home, he could be seen alert and interested, sitting up next to the driver in the cab of the lorry, long front legs braced like pokers against the swerves.

While Roderick counted the days until the Easter holidays and with the house tidied and prepared once more for summer visitors, Miranda and I flew to Dakar.

This capital city boasted university, Roman Catholic cathedral, zoo and sandy beaches amongst its amenities. It would have made an agreeable posting. Our destination, however, was several miles up the coast: a small town named St Louis.

John welcomed the idea of living and working in a former French colony and he particularly liked the fact that so many Senegalese spoke excellent French, coping manfully with the subjunctive in their everyday speech.

Collecting Miranda and me at the airport, he drove us to the Dakar home of the First Secretary and his wife. They'd offered us hospitality for the night before we set off for St Louis.

While Miranda sat on the bed clutching her pink blanket I unpacked the overnight cases, straightening up in dismay when John announced,

"We've been invited to dinner this evening by the British Ambassador."

"Oh very funny!"

"No, it's true. And I've brought the linen suit Anna made you in Teheran, so you've got something to wear."

The last thing I felt ready for after the long journey was having to make polite conversation with important people. I was also self-conscious about a rash on my hands and wrists, the result of too much contact with Tide soap powder. Nevertheless, I had to concede that this was not the sort of invitation one could easily turn down.

Like her brother, Miranda was a sociable child and made no objection to being baby-sat by the First Secretary's wife.

Greeted on the steps of the Embassy by the Ambassador and his wife we found we were to be the only guests. But the serenity of the splendid house with its high ceilings, the dignity and efficiency of the servants and homeliness of our hosts all combined to put us at our ease. After a pre-dinner gin and tonic I quite forgot the state of my hands.

In John's new Peugeot we drove next day to St Louis, a journey of several hours. This small fishing town stands on both sides of an estuary into which flows the Senegal river. The commercial centre of St Louis occupies part of a long, narrow peninsula bordering the Atlantic. Connecting it with the inland side on which we were to live was a six-span bridge. The road to the bridge ran along the water-front, a pleasing scene with its palm trees, shrubs and grass, but less agreeable when approached from down-wind. Public latrines overhung the edge of the water and the sewage had nowhere to go but into the estuary.

Our flat was cool, with two bedrooms and living room down one side. A corridor separated this area from a spacious terrace. The wall between corridor and terrace was made of latticed, white-washed concrete, the small gaps letting in air but not the rays of the sun. For a month or two the terrace was the place where Miranda and I spent most of the day. While I knitted or sewed she took her trolley of bricks for walks, avoiding the troughs of plants that provided welcome touches of green against the dazzling white of the walls. Sitting under the beach umbrella provided by our landlady I considered St Louis wasn't going to be such a bad place. I had yet to learn the reason why none of the other expatriate wives whose husbands worked for the FAO would leave Dakar for this backwater.

The owner of our building was a woman of generous proportions, her ebony colouring enhanced by the blue and silver of a garment reaching down to her ankles, the whole outfit complemented by a matching turban. On special occasions, women magnificently dressed in gold or silver taffeta swept along the dusty street below our flat, bound no doubt for some St Louis version of Ascot or perhaps simply to join in a feast of mutton to celebrate the Muslim new year. Sometimes we'd see a camel stalk past, its rider enveloped in dark blue, head swathed in a turban, only the eyes visible. This would be a tribesman from next-door Mauritania.

Islam was the dominant religion in Senegal; the few Christians mostly Roman Catholic, although a tiny minority of protestants had established a small church a mile or two out of St Louis. At Sunday service I spoke to an English missionary couple recently arrived from Portugese West Africa. They were resigned to the fact that they only saw their children (looked after in England by members of their denomination) every three years but were equally saddened by their lack of conversions. In spite of this they had no intention of joining the Baptish church in St Louis. They planned to build one of their own. This was sad indeed.

CHAPTER 2

Roderick joined us for three weeks at Easter and the terrace continued to be the main living area. Miranda played in the sand-pit put together for her by the local carpenter who'd constructed her sturdy cot, while Roderick made good use of the carpentry skills he'd acquired at school. He also spent informative time in the kitchen. Our cook, a disdainful but efficient young man whom we called Jalou, liked having someone to talk to and this helped Roderick's French to take a turn for the better. More attractive for Roderick than improving his French, however, was to observe the lethal properties of the Shell fly-killer hanging in the kitchen over the work-top. Any fly touching the yellow slab succumbed instantly to its poison.

It was while we were in St Louis that we became acquainted with another insect repellent. Named "Moon Tiger Mosquito Coils" by its Japanese makers, this totally environment-friendly product kept our bedroom free of mosquitoes. Smelling of joss-sticks the substance burned for eight hours, its smell anathema to mosquitoes. The label on the box of coils assured the user that:-

"The Million of the final consumers for Mosquito Coils are completely satisfied with MOON TIGER BRAND ...for its fine quality. ...Coils are always available for indoor, outdoor, on vacation trips, at a picnic, whiling sleeping... If you make use of Moon Tiger Coils you can enjoy restful and peaceful nights without being troubled by indiscriminate mosquitoes."

We came to bless this modest but effective product and I preserved the endearingly-worded label in my scrapbook.

Picnics became once more a regular feature for us. A typical one took us up a tributary of the Senegal river. Roderick found a tree to climb while we lazed on the grass watching a small fishing boat as it was propelled across the water by a figure in the stern.

Miranda's second birthday in April provided another diversion, her brother insisting she must have a decorated cake. This I ordered from a Senegalese baker in town, asking him in French to pipe "le nom Miranda" onto the icing in pink letters. When later we called to collect the cake Roderick and I were interested to note that on it the baker had carefully written the words "LE NOM MIRANDA".

A few days after this and loaded with a bag of mangoes, Roderick was driven by his Dad to Dakar airport for the return to school.

By the month of May the temperature had risen until it was impossible to make use of the terrace. Once overhead the sun forced us to stay inside. This made the days long although Miranda was content to trundle her toys up and down the corridor, stopping to exchange greetings with the small green parrot, Zik II, as he sat on top of his cage. Sometimes Zik would climb down to join her in a game of marbles. He also shared her preference for the colour red. If he spotted a small red plastic toy on the floor he'd snatch it up if he could reach it before she did.

The high spot of the afternoon for Miranda came with our daily visit to the landlady's yard where she kept a chicken in a run. The chicken and Miranda would contemplate each other for a minute or two. Then, satisfied, Miranda would take my hand and back upstairs we'd go.

Sometimes I drove with her in the VW Beetle past the smells of the water-front latrines and over the bridge into town where both European and African shops were to be found. The Senegalese were polite but not warm; we had no encounters of any significance, either pleasant or hostile.

I found a shop run by a Frenchwoman who stocked dress materials imported from France. Making clothes for myself and Miranda helped keep boredom at bay and trivial events also became important, as for instance when it was time to open a new packet of Bonux soap powder. Inside would be a free gift, sometimes a toy, and once I found a well-made screwdriver. I could see that Jalou coveted this but I hung onto it. Loneliness was making me disagreeable.

The lack of adult companionship day after day was in fact doing bad things to my spirits; when John came home for lunch one day I startled him by bursting into tears. (I hadn't known I was going to do this but the last straw may have been the drab colour of the knitting I held in my lap. Mud-colour was the only shade the shop had been able to come up with).

"I don't think I can stand this place much longer! I'm going round the bend. Could Miranda and I go home?"

Although this was the first serious complaint I'd made, John wasn't altogether surprised. He'd heard from colleagues the views held by their wives on St Louis as a place to live.

"Right. But you'll have to stay for six months at least or the FAO won't pay your fare."

This could be borne. At least I could start counting the days. And the knowledge that in six weeks' time I'd be escaping from this deadly existence helped make the delay tolerable.

The weeks crept by until the last day when we set off for Dakar at 4 o'clock in the morning. As the sun rose I saw for the last time the ungainly baobab trees casting shade over the russet-coloured sandy earth, the women with pots on their heads making for the nearest water supply. Farewell, French-speaking Africa.

Waving goodbye to John who had four more months of St Louis to put up with, I climbed aboard the Air France plane with Miranda clutching my skirt; in one hand I held a small case and in the other Zik in a makeshift cage.

CHAPTER 3

As we flew northwards I reflected on our future. Since he had no reason to suppose he'd find another contract within a UN agency, John had decided to take a business studies course at the Norwich Tech. This would give him the paper qualifications that in spite of his five years with UN agencies he still lacked. While he studied in the evenings, I would work as a secretary during the day.

John would of course miss being an international civil servant – he had after all done it rather well – but what bliss it would be to live in our own house within easy reach of family, friends and Roderick's school.

This programme – appealing to me and not in the least to John as it transpired – occupied my thoughts during the long flight. Miranda in the meantime enjoyed being airborne far too much to think of snatching any sleep, however badly needed.

Landing at London Airport we found ourselves in the midst of the August crush and her expression became anxious. Great was her distress when I told her I couldn't pick her up as I had the overnight case and Zik to carry.

From the arrivals section we pushed our way downstairs to collect suitcases from the conveyor belt. With horror I realised one of my hands was free. Where was the small case? Back upstairs we hurried and there, containing cash and travellers' cheques, was the blue case patiently waiting on the floor where I'd left it. Down to the luggage hall we returned, Miranda by this time in tears as she clutched the hem of my skirt. A porter put our cases onto a trolley.

"Oh you don't want to waste money on a taxi – that'd cost you £5 – take the coach!"

However, persuaded that Miranda was nearing the end of her endurance after thirteen hours without sleep, he led us to a rank where we climbed into the soothing interior of a taxi.

Once more the haven of the Great Eastern Hotel, Liverpool Street, enveloped us; and after the usual sandwiches and tea, it was cloth over cage for Zik, bath and bed for Miranda and me.

The two-hour train journey to Norwich the following day lasted forever. Miranda's fatigue made it impossible for her to settle and there were protests and tears, causing much lip-tightening amongst the other occupants of the carriage. At last after a 25-mile taxi ride from Thorpe Station we reached Rose Cottage and stepped thankfully into its cool interior.

I loved this small house with its thick flint-and-brick walls, pantiled roof and box hedge in front that gave off an aromatic smell in the August sunshine. Indulging in anthropomorphic fantasy I sensed the house was pleased to have us back.

For a treat Roderick, Miranda and I were to have had a week's holiday at Butlin's, but for many weeks following our return Miranda continued to suffer from the effects of the gruelling journey; her bouts of rage and tears, something new in her, convinced me that to take her on holiday would be a disaster. This was a huge disappointment for Roderick but he didn't reproach his sister. By the time she'd recovered the summer holidays were almost over and we never got to our holiday camp.

Neither did we become ordinary British tax-payers. When John joined us for Christmas he'd made up his mind that life in Britain was not for him. Starting in January we'd have an eight-week spell on the Costa del Sol so he could learn Spanish and thereby improve his employment prospects with the UN. He was far from having given up hope of working for them again.

Disappointed though I was I couldn't pretend this change of course had taken me by surprise. John simply wasn't cast in the mould of country Englishman going off every morning on his bike or in the Morris Minor to his studies and later no doubt to a white-collar job. I should never have gone to Nigeria as a single woman if I'd wanted a UK existence.

"Don't put your daughter on the stage, Mrs Worthington" could have been paraphrased as "Don't let your daughter go abroad, Mrs Stewart" – not that I would have taken any notice of what my mother had to say on the subject and not that she minded my going away.

Oh well, eight weeks in the sun will be pleasant, I reflected. In due course, with Roderick back at school to play soccer on bleak January afternoons, John and I set off in our small car, Miranda stretched out on the pile of suitcases at the back. Two days later after an over-night stop in Seville we arrived at Fuengirola.

Waiting to greet us and hand over the flat keys was the English owner of the small apartment building overlooking beach and blue sea. Our flat, furnished in folksy style with rush-seated chairs and much painted woodwork, was flooded with late afternoon sun.

Before unpacking I walked down to the beach with Miranda clutching bucket and spade, but we didn't stay. Wherever we put our feet a sticky black tarry substance stuck to our shoes. Clean-up operations on the beach would no doubt get going with the approach of the season, but until that time the sand must be avoided. And next morning the rain started. Except for brief intervals, it didn't let up during the whole of our stay.

After breakfast each morning John went off to his lessons. Miranda was happy 'reading' her Richard Scarry books when not standing on a chair to do the washing-up over and over again. Much water landed on the floor but I was past caring. In the afternoons the three of us went for damp walks on the scrubby hillsides and I quickly got through the thirty novels supplied by the owner of the flat.

Home again in Briningham with his Spanish more fluent, John didn't hang about for long but set off for Geneva to see what was what in the job line. In no time he'd rung me to break the glad tidings of the offer of a desk job in the Palais des Nations. (Goodo, I don't think). Once the school term had started for Roderick, Miranda and I were to join him. I must also find an au pair since it would be necessary for me to get a full-time job as well. One salary would not go far in Geneva.

None of this thrilled me, especially the thought of having to leave Miranda with someone else during the day. I'd had enough of that when Roderick was small. However, the time for disobedience had not yet arrived.

With the help of Universal Aunts I engaged an au pair and shortly afterwards John's and my final posting as a couple began in the bland city overlooking Lac Leman. When doing time in the Congo we and other expatriates working for UN agencies regarded Geneva as a golden place where everything was civilised and free from menacing goings-on, but in fact our sojourn there saw the beginning of the end of our marriage. The Ethiopian army officer in Luluabourg had in our case been speaking prophetically when he'd observed how many UN marriages came unstuck.

Although on the one hand I hadn't taken to the life we'd led in a variety of countries all those years, moving so frequently from one place to another, I do on the other hand relish the memory of many of our experiences. Parading them across my mind has kept me entertained on many a long car drive.

Stewart Marker may sometimes have been ill-advised, falling in when she should have pulled back, but at times she Saw Life and some of her adventures might well have impressed Blyton's Famous Five.